D1479318

5332829

THE NATURE AND USE OF RITUAL:

The Great Christian Documents and Traditional Blue-Prints for Human and Spiritual Growth

Peter Roche de Coppens

BL
600
.R62
1979

University Press of America™

Copyright © 1979 by

University Press of America, Inc.™

4710 Auth Place, S.E., Washington D.C. 20023

All rights reserved

Printed in the United States of America

ISBN: 0-8191-0341-1

— The Library
INTERNATIONAL CHRISTIAN
GRADUATE UNIVERSITY

TABLE OF CONTENTS

Chapter
   I.   INTRODUCTION...................................   1

  II.   THE GREAT WORK: ITS NATURE, ESSENCE, AND
            REALIZATION............................... 13

 III.   SPIRITUALITY AND THE SPIRITUAL TRADITION......... 21

  IV.   THE SEVEN FUNDAMENTALS AND THE PRIMORDIAL
            TRADITION................................. 33

   V.   DIVINE NAMES: THEIR NATURE AND USE............. 39

  VI.   THE SIGN OF THE CROSS: ITS NATURE AND USE....... 53

 VII.   THE LORD'S PRAYER: ITS NATURE AND USE........... 67

VIII.   THE NICENE CREED: ITS NATURE AND USE............ 78

  IX.   THE BEATITUDES: THEIR NATURE AND USE........... 86

   X.   THE HAIL MARY: ITS NATURE AND USE.............. 93

  XI.   THE TEN COMMANDMENTS: THEIR NATURE AND USE...... 98

 XII.   CONCLUSION: THE NATURE AND USE OF RITUAL........ 119

....

FOOTNOTES... 125

APPENDIX: A.   THE HUMAN PSYCHE........................ 126
           B.   THE INTUITION.......................... 132
           C.   SYMBOLISM.............................. 137
           D.   THE TREE OF LIFE AND THE
                    PSYCHOSPIRITUAL CENTERS........... 143

BIBLIOGRAPHY... 145

32114

CHAPTER I

INTRODUCTION

Every age has what has aptly been called a <u>Zeitgeist</u>, a spirit or ethos characterizing that age; an intellectual soul reflecting the central preoccupations, fears, experiences, and aspirations of the people who live, think, and work in it. Every <u>Zeitgeist</u>, moreover, has what Lewis Mumford has perceptively called "dominant themes" and "emergent themes." Dominant themes are those values and norms, those beliefs and aspirations which have been institutionalized by the culture at large and which are reflected in the consciousness, strivings, and daily lives of the majority. Emergent themes, on the other hand, are those new assumptions, ideals, and aspirations which are proposed and espoused by a creative minority. This creative and "evolutionary" minority, dissatisfied with the current realities and opportunities offered by their society, are intuiting, seeking, and laboring for something that, for them, is "higher" and more genuinely satisfying than what they can find in the world in which they are living.

The dominant themes of our age are, basically and briefly, the questions of national and international peace, of social justice and injustice, of social reform or revolution, of material success and affluence, of science, secular humanism, and global industrialism. The most dynamic emergent themes of our epoch are, on the other hand, those dealing with an ecology of the earth, of the psyche, and of the spirit; the question of the meaning and purpose of man, life, and the universe; of human growth and self-expression, of personal and collective self-actualization and Self-realization. They are, essentially, the old but perennial spiritual quest in modern dress and form: that we are unfinished animals summoned to unfold astonishing possibilities, to further unfold our human consciousness and to actualize our human and spiritual faculties.

Having explored and conquerred the outer physical world, harnessed the raw materials and the physical energies of nature, through science and technology, and developed an urban and industrial civilization which now reigns supreme in most advanced nations, but having failed to find either a lasting inner or outer peace, satisfying justice or goodness, true beauty or genuine purpose, an ever greater number of people are now turning,

1

in their unending and ever-renewed search for happiness, toward an exploration of the inner worlds of the psyche, towards the latent energies and faculties of the mind, and towards the unexplored heights and potentialities of the spirit.

To an outer and physical science and technology of the material universe, to an extraverted preoccupation with nature and a higher standard of living, must now correspond and be slowly and painfully developed an inner and psychic "science" and "technology" of the human psyche, an introverted investigation of man himself and of his meaning, purpose, and destiny. For the truly fundamental and universal questions that have always faced man and that will always confront him, especially when he slowly awakens from his mental amnesia, from his emotiona narcosis, and from his spiritual slumber, are no more answered today than they were a few centuries ago before the advent of the modern age. In fact, because of the slow decay of those social institutions which provided ready-made answers to these questions, they are perhaps even less satisfactorily answered than they were a few centuries ago. Yet man's present psychological stirrings and conflicts, and his existential dilemmas and trials are now pressing down upon him, perhaps more acutely than before, to find or fashion viable answers to them or to perish both psychologically and socially. The need to find answers to these central questions is great indeed; more than great, it is desperate; it is possibly the central need of our times and so many people, each in his own way, are responding to it.

Briefly put, these great questions are:

A. The riddle of the Sphinx: What is man? What am I? Where do I come from and where am I going? Why am I here on earth? What am I supposed to do here? How should I live?

B. The enigma of life: What is life? Where does it come from and where is it going? What is its purpose and how do I fit in that purpose?

C. The puzzle of the universe: What is the universe? Where does it come from and where is it going? Who or what created it and for what purpose? And how do I fit in this purpose?

Ever since the Renaissance, and particularly the Enlightenment, philosophy first and then science have pointed to the physical universe, to external nature, as being the guardian of the ultimate answer to these questions and have suggested that objective empirical observation, logical reasoning, and much experimentation would ultimately provide meaningful and satisfying answers. But, alas, they have not! The great promise of the Renaissance and of the Enlightenment has not been realized;

the logico-experimental method has not provided deeper meanings, larger syntheses, and a life more abundant for larger numbers of people. All it has produced is more material affluence for some and more dehumanized misery for others, much greater power and physical energies but much less wisdom and goodness to use these powers and energies constructively. Thus the creative potential and the exploration of this cultural approach are now nearly exhausted, with the substantial answers no where in sight, while our material resources have been ruthlessly exploited and depleted, and human conflicts, both at the intra and at the interpsychic levels have reached the point where a major conflagration could easily explode, destroying our sanity and our civilization. Thus it is not only understandable but also imperative that many people, particularly the young, the most concerned, the most sensitive, and the brightest should now turn to other cultural premises for possible answers--that they should turn towards the inner space, the vertical dimension of introspection and meditation, in the desperate hope to wrest from the depths and the heights of their own being those long sought and repressed answers which have become so crucial for our very physical, let alone psychological, survival. Thus the axiological and philosophical foundation of our culture are again changing and we are witnessing both the "death" of an old world and the "birth" of a new world.

This reminds me of a game I was once asked to play and which puzzled me and frustrated me terribly until I found the simple answer by going from the horizontal to the vertical dimension (how to form 4 triangles and a square with 4 matches... answer: build a pyramid!). Another interesting example is the scientific search for the origins of life and consciousness in matter through various observations and analyses. The biological organism of an animal is endowed with life (as shown by its transformation, growth, and motility). To grasp the secret of that life, empirical scientists have isolated one key organ of that organism, say the heart or the brain. This organ was then disected into its component parts (reductionistic, analytical method), the cells. To wrest the secret of life from these cells, these were then looked at through the "optic" of inorganic chemistry revealing an organized atomic structure which, when further analyzed in terms of nuclear physics, revealed millions of subatomic particles--protons, neutrons, and electrons. These, when even further analyzed, vanished altogether into quantum wave-particle probabilities, doing away not only with organized life but with matter itself! By using the logico-experimental method and its reductionistic method, irriversible thresholds are crossed (consciousness to life, life to matter, matter into probability waves) which, not only do not yield the answers that are sought, but which even obliterate the dimension and level of organization which is being investigated! Clearly then, the answers must be looked for "above" and not "below," in the higher reaches of human consciousness and not in matter.

The "rediscovery" and exploration of the inner spaces, of the latent energies and faculties of the psyche, and of the dormant potentialities and powers of the spirit has produced, in the second half of the 20th century, a very wide variety of heterogeneous results and approaches. Very different types of persons and groups were drawn to this quest by very different motives. On the one hand, we have the established religions with their ancient traditions, their symbols, rituals, and ceremonies which are repositories of the Hidden Wisdom and of the Mysteries, but which have lost, for the most part, their ancient mystical and practical explanations and applications that were based in an oral tradition. Thus they have failed to develop a practical interpretation of their tradition that fits the needs and the consciousness of our age. Precious treasures of the Hidden Wisdom can, indeed, be found there but, alas, not their meaningful explanation of integrated practical exercises. What organized religions have is a body and a spirit of the sacred traditions; what they lack is a soul: a practical and meaningful interpretation that can be accepted and used by the educated members of our society and by our searching youth who need high ideals and a sound discipline so badly.

On the other hand, we have parapsychological and extrasensory research using, most of the time, the methods and approaches of the natural sciences. Consequently, this approach is getting lost in a maze of statistics, tests, and psychophysiological research and psychical phenomena which may, indeed, be sensational and startling, but which totally lacks the essence and the spirit of what is being investigated. Both subjects and researchers are, generally, psychodynamically and spiritually untrained and indescriminately selected, lacking the discipline and the frame of reference necessary to be truly productive in this field.

Finally, we have guardians of ancient and not-so-ancient esoteric traditions who veil their insights and teachings behind a nearly impenetrable and, many times, outdated language and symbolism, and who keep whatever truth and techniques they have by imponent but largely sterile oaths of silence within the walls of their temples. And we also have the "freaks" and other "drop-outs" of the "consciousness circuit" who travel from center to center, from guru to guru, and from one tradition or fad to another. One day, they sample TM, TA, or Zazen, another astral projection, aura-reading, or Eckankar; for one season, it is yoga or Buddhism that is in, for the next bioenergetics, gestalt therapy, or witchcraft.

The genuine esoteric orders do exist, to be sure, but they do not advertise and their members, who use a great deal of discretion and a good dose of common sense, can only be recognized, here and there, by their vital and dynamic personalities, their kindness and penetrating wisdom, and the many people they have and are helping.

In this jungle of confusion, this quicksand of counter-
feit and instant wisdom, and this maze of materialistic analyses
and psychophysiological disection, where can the earnest, sincere, and mature seeker turn? This is a truly fundamental
question which I have asked myself for many years and which has
guided me through many adventures, and even more misadventures,
in the labyrinth of the occult, mystical, spiritual, and self-
development circuit. The carefully weighed answers I would
give to this question, drawn from my own personal experiences,
trials and errors, is:

a. First and foremost, this person should turn to himself and
his own personal growth and development, purification and
consecration. He should acquire systematic self-knowledge,
then self-mastery, and finally self-realization. There is
simply no substitute for these "simple fundamentals" and
they must be acquired, however painfully and slowly, through
some form of humanistic therapy or auto-psychosynthesis and,
preferably, with some form of wise and loving guidance by a
qualified person. This is all the more important in an age,
such as ours, when external authorities of all sorts are
slowly disintegrating and contradicting each other. Our age
is truly the age in which earnest and mature seekers are
compelled to turn inwards, to undertake the "inward journey
to their Source," to seek refuge in the "Inner Fortress,"
and guidance from the Inner Light, as a pluralistic and
anarchic atmosphere prevails in the outer world.

b. Second, he should turn to the sacred traditions of the past
as embodied by the great World Religions, on the one hand, and,
to the valid Mystery Schools or Esoteric Orders, on the other--
for both mutually complement and reinforce each other.

c. Third, he should turn to the guidance and the living example
of another human being who has proven his "wisdom" by what
he is, by how he lives, and by what he does rather than
merely by what he says or preaches.

d. Fourth, he should turn to the best of modern science and
integrate what he can learn here with the former in a
creative and vivifying synthesis; for science is slowly
but surely advancing towards the discovery of the inner
spaces, the latent powers of the mind, and the realization
of the spiritual realms and energies.

Science, here, should be understood as the method of direct,
personal observation and experience as opposed to the method of
relying on the words, discoveries, and experiences of others, of
external authorities. This new approach is very important and
constitutes a central and distinctive feature of the New Age:
ancient revelation, wisdom, and spiritual teachings must now be
expressed in a "scientific form," i.e., the spirit of the Ageless

Wisdom must be provided with a new "form," the form corresponding to our age which, being essentially a mental age, can best be expressed in "scientific" language, methodology, and experience.

The word "science," I feel, should be specifically defined in the sense in which I am using it; for, otherwise, it could lead to further confusion and controversy. To me, this word means basically two things:

1. An objective, systematic, and precise study of any area or aspect of reality, whether in the microcosm or in the macrocosm, which is grounded either in direct observation or in direct experience. The difference between observation and experience is also crucial for there are many aspects of reality (e.g. ideas, emotions, states of consciousness, love, and enlightenment) which, unlike material things or behavior, cannot be seen but which can be experienced. Thus, while the natural sciences deal more with the observable part of the empirical world, the human and social sciences deal more with the humanly experienced side of the same "empirical world."

   Another insight and realization, which are absolutely fundamental for the New Age, is that the so-called "empirical world" (i.e. those aspects and facets of the world which are open to human observation and human experience) is not static and absolute but dynamic and relative; relative to man's evolutionary status, level of consciousness, and personal development. Man is, indeed, the first and the ultimate knowledge-getting-instrument and thus perception and understanding are completely dependent upon his level of consciousness and development which have many unsuspected levels of emergence. Besides his 5 senses, which are quantitatively extended by sophisticated modern machines such as telescopes and microscopes, there are also latent senses in man that can be awakened and activated and which will then reveal new and qualitatively different aspects of reality (e.g. clairvoyance, clairaudience, and spiritual enlightenment). Likewise, there are also many different, higher and lower, levels of consciousness in man than the ones he normally functions in and which can greatly expand his domain of direct, personal experience on a qualitative continuum.

2. It implies working with the method developed by Francis Bacon from which, alas, many of our modern, dogmatic, and close-minded "sciences" have departed to a large extent, falling into new "metaphysics," "delusions," and finally even "superstitions" (e.g. materialism, positivism, behaviorism). Simply put, the method advocated by Bacon

operates in such a way as to clear, or purify, the mind
from many conscious or unconscious "idols," or distortions,
which involuntarily clutter it and distort its perceptions
and conclusions. Bacon listed 4 major "idols" which, unfortunately, are still very much with us today and which
distort the views of laymen and scientists alike, namely:

a. Idols of the cave which he defined as "prejudices due
    to the nature of the individual," i.e. unconscious and
    subconscious drives and impulses originating in our
    biopsychic nature and in our character.

b. Idols of the tribe which he defined as "prejudices due
    to the customs of the human race," i.e. influences and
    impulses originating in the collective unconscious and
    subconscious, and in the character of our sociocultural
    milieu which, subliminally, affects man's mind and per-
    ceptions.

c. Idols of the market place which he defined as "prejudices
    due to the use of words," i.e. semantical distortions
    and social definitions which slant or distort the true
    nature of certain words and symbols, confusing or mixing
    up the 3 different languages of everyday speech, of science,
    and of religion.

d. Idols of the theater which he defined as "prejudices
    due to the influence of great names," i.e. the compelling
    and, sometimes, distorting influence of established
    "authorities."

These idols, or distortions, he claimed, should be replaced
by direct and precise observations, experiments, and analyses.

A very interesting convergence and consensus which is now
slowly emerging between the ancient sacred traditions and the
most advanced thrusts of modern science is the emphasis that both
give to an alteration, transformation, and expansion of human
consciousness. This, they both assert, is truly fundamental for
any presently adequate knowledge system and understanding of
reality, whether objective, in the world, or subjective, within
man. Both approaches recognize that, somehow, human consciousness,
in its normal functioning, operates on 3 levels, namely:

a. The physical or sensorial level.

b. The emotional or affective level.

c. The mental or cognitive level.

Both approaches also concur that, on these 3 levels,
human consciousness is unable to penetrate to the core and true
nature of reality, both in the microcosm, in man, and in the

8

macrocosm, in the world. Thus, that a new and qualitatively
different level of consciousness, i.e. "enlightened" or
"spiritual" consciousness, is absolutely necessary for true
science to continue its onward march into the nature of reality
and for man to take his next evolutionary step in the present
era; that this new level of consciousness needs deliberate
and extended work on self to be achieved; and that, unlike the
first levels, it is not a "free gift of nature" but, rather,
a self-acquired fruit of art or labor. The old religious injunction; "Seek ye first the Kingdom of Heaven (i.e. a new,
spiritual level of consciousness) and all these things shall
be added unto you" (i.e. then you will be able to truly know
yourself and your purpose on earth, and to understand reality)
gets at the very heart of this matter in its own characteristic
manner--which is to use appropriate symbolism or analogies.

One of the most fundamental questions for all earnest and
serious seekers, and the very starting point of their true quest,
is, therefore: How can I alter and expand my human consciousness
so as to achieve at least some valid flashes of this new state
of consciousness to guide me and inspire me in my quest? While
there are many routes and approaches that lead to different altered and expanded states of consciousness, in all of these we
can recognize and select certain basic elements which are:

a. Obtaining the proper knowledge of the effective means to do
so in a safe and balanced way.

b. Unfolding the motivation and the energies to apply effectively
these means and to carry out the work required.

c. Developing the right motives and judgment for doing so and
then using in a positive and constructive manner the new
energies and faculties which will be forthcoming.

The answer given to this great quest for "rebirth" (i.e. an
effective transformation and expansion of consciousness) by
the sacred traditions and now, increasingly more also by the
humanistic, transpersonal, height schools of modern psychology,
is the fusion and synthesis of worship (the love of God) with
service (the love of man). For these, in fact, constitute the
central axes of any genuine human and spiritual development
which can be placed on a vertical and horizontal set of coor-
dinates.

Around these are also grounded the twin aims of self-
actualization: psychosocial work aiming at the development of
the personality, and Self-realization: psychospiritual work
aiming at discovering one's spiritual Self and aligning one's
consciousness with it. Whatever approach or system is used,
these are the "basic fundamentals" which must be confronted and
slowly acquired and internalized.

Worship, in its inner structure, contains a "male" and a "female" polarity, the first being Ritual and its proper use, while the second is Silence and its proper achievement. Service, too, includes a "male" and a "female" polarity: actively helping others to effectively enhance their being and lives and allowing them to help and enrich themselves.

The present study will focus mainly upon Ritual and its proper use, at the theoretical level, and its specific development and application in the "Seven Fundamentals" of the Christian tradition--although these may equally well be applied to other "Fundamentals" of other religious traditions. It is the ritualistic use of these seven fundamentals--which contain a true "science" and "art" of human and spiritual development--that both the necessary knowledge and the proper motivation, and the correct motives and judgment can be found and slowly unfolded through specific practical exercises. Each of these fundamentals contains symbols, glyphs, and practical exercises which are designed to set in motion the "intuitive faculty," to bring about a genuine breakthrough of the superconscious into the conscious, and to lead to the dawning of spiritual consciousness. Each demands the proper use and development of specific functions of the psyche through its appropriate process, leads to the psychological preparation necessary for the inrush of the new energies, and brings, as its by-product, an emergent knowledge and understanding which will guide the seeker in his spiritual adventure.

These psychospiritual "calesthenics," however, are not a substitute for a clean, constructive, moral, and balanced natural life which should precede and accompany them. This is clearly and explicitly pointed out by one of the oldest spiritual systems known to mankind, the Yoga Sutras of Patanjali. Here 7 steps or stages are developed: Yama-Niyama, Asana, Pranayama, Pratyahara, Dharana, Dhyana, and Samadhi. Yama-Niyama are the basic "dos" and "do nots," or an ethical attitude and practice towards life and others which precedes, and should precede, all the later phases. Asana and Pranayama are respectively physical training and breathing exercises, leading to a balanced life. Pratyahara, Dharana, and Dhyana are respectively Concentration, Meditation, and Contemplation. While Samadhi is spiritual Illumination or Union with God, the culminating phase and the final object of the whole system. Our investigation of Ritual and its proper use deals specifically with Pratyahara, Dharana, and Dhyana, leading eventually to Samadhi. All too often, unfortunately, contemporary seekers forget or by-pass the Yama-Niyama stage and, sometimes, also the Asana-Pranayama phase with very deleterious effects for their emotional and mental health and for their human relationships. These stages are sine qua non for the mature seeker and cannot be neglected or by-passed without reaping severe consequences.

In the conscious and proper use of Ritual, the will is developed through the process of <u>concentration</u>, i.e. focusing one's whole attention and awareness upon a chosen subject, or point, at the exclusion of all other things, or turning one's mind into a "magnifying glass," and, later, through the process of <u>affirmation</u>. Thinking is developed through the process of <u>meditation</u>, in its reflective, receptive, contemplative, and creative aspects, bringing in its wake much additional knowledge by way of new associations, correspondences, and relationships. Feeling is developed through the process of <u>devotion</u> and <u>adoration</u>, i.e. exhalting and purifying one's emotions by focusing them devotionally upon the Divine within. Finally imagination is developed through the process of <u>visualization</u> which, again, focuses upon the Divine within with images and archetypes that act as psychic channels of expression.

As the symbols, petitions, and the whole glyph of the given fundamental is deciphered, in terms of its various meanings, correspondences, and implications on various "planes," or states of consciousness, and as the various practical exercises it contains are revealed and properly understood and applied, then comes the final and culminating phase--its <u>theurgic use</u> in <u>invocation</u> and <u>evocation</u> through which human aspiration is answered by spiritual inspiration, and the breakthrough between the superconscious and the conscious is established and experientially realized.

Schematically formulated, the working procedure is to:

1. Write down the chosen fundamental and break it down in terms of its component parts, i.e. its symbols.

2. Develop the will and the power of concentration by concentrating first on one symbol, then on one petition, and finally on the whole document.

3. Develop thinking and meditation by meditating first on one symbol, then on one petition, and finally on the whole document to decipher its inner meanings, correspondences, and practical applications. Each new meaning, association, and discovery should then be filed away in the subconscious memory for later use.

4. Amplify and exhalt feeling and "make prayer come alive" by directing all your love and emotions first on one symbol, then on one petition, and finally on the whole document, to progressively generate and express greater love for the Divine within and the Great Work.

5. Train and cultivate imagination and visualization by visualizing (and letting new images and symbols flow before your mental "screen" of vision) first one symbol, then one petition, and finally the whole document.

6. File away, both in your work-book and in your mind, all the practical implications and exercises discovered thus far.

7. Finally, use one symbol, one petition, or the whole document, to practice one and then the other exercises that have been "revealed" by synthesizing and converging concentration, meditation, devotion, and visualization into a pointed, upward-thrusting <u>invocation</u>; wait for an answer, a response, an awakening, or the ensuing <u>evocation</u>. After this has occurred, record the event and the experience you just went through in your work-book.

The practical exercises, the invocations and its following evocations, can be used for one's self as well as for others, for specific as for general purposes, to awaken a given psycho-spiritual center or the whole Tree of Life, for healing or for personality work. Their applications are practically limitless and deepen as one continues with the work and achieves more advanced stages. The faculties, powers, and new states of consciousness thus trained and unfolded can be used for worship as well as for service, for spiritual as well as for psychological development, for "sacred" as well as for "profane" purposes. Engaged in long enough and with enough persistence, they will gradually lead to the development of a new state of consciousness and being, to a new personality and a new life, permeating and affecting all of one's interpersonal relations and all of one's activities. Integrated with the other aspects of the Great Work, with "living the Life," with a proper and personal rhythm of Prayer, Work, and Relaxation, and with constructive activities and a rich and satisfying social life, this training will, eventually, lead one to true Samadhi--to spiritual Illumination or "Union with God" which is the greatest and ultimate purpose of life on earth and man's true destiny.

The core of this book and the following chapters are made up of a series of integrated lectures which I gave at different times and places, and finally as an interrelated Seminar on the topics of Worship, Ritual, and the Seven Fundamentals. Thus each chapter is both an autonomous unit and a sequential step in an organic process. Each contains a theoretical development as well as practical applications of Ritual, its nature, uses, and possibilities. Each embodies vital principles, exercises, and actual psychospiritual "calesthentics" which, taken together, form a complete curriculum in human and spiritual development. Rather than re-editing these lectures to streamline them, I have decided to leave them as they are. This both to facilitate their independent use by the reader and to show the various steps and sequential development of my exploration of them.

Let the reader keep in mind at all times, however, that
it is up to him to do the required work, to train his faculties,
psychological functions, and to progressively unveil the various meanings, correspondences, and associations these "fundamentals" contain and to discover their practical applications.
The work of the interpretation and "deciphering" of these
"fundamentals" and sets of symbols is merely the beginning of
a long Path; it is not a substitute for the reader's own med-
itations and work; it is merely a simple and practical example
of what can and should be done, of how this work can be carried
out, and of the great rewards and self-growth it can bring.

CHAPTER II

THE GREAT WORK: ITS NATURE, ESSENCE, AND REALIZATION

Ever since man unfolded the power of thinking, of reflecting upon the nature of life, of the universe, and of himself, he has, consciously or unconsciously, become involved with the Great Work. In all places where human culture developed and at all times, the more serious and concerned thinkers have become interested in and have begun to work upon what came to be known as the Great Work or Magnum Opus. At the core of what has been called the Ancient or Ageless Wisdom, the Hagia Sophia or Philosophia Perennis, we can find the Great Work just as we can find it in the heart of all true religion and philosophy, for it is indeed the most important and the highest human achievement. Countless books, essays, and elucidations of the Great Work have been offered by different traditions, schools, and organizations. The purpose of this brief sketch of the Great Work will be an attempt to get at its substance and to describe in as simple and practical terms as possible what is its nature, essence, and purpose and how it can be realized by modern persons who are earnest seekers aspiring to more in life than what their culture and the example of their fellow-men offers.

In all religious, metaphysical, philosophical, and even esoteric traditions, we find that the Great Work, in its essence, has always stood for three basic endeavors: the study of man, his conscious improvement, and the realization of his ultimate perfection. This is the true heart and core of the Great Work whatever its manifold external expressions, aspects, and degrees may be. At the foundation of the Great Work we find, for example, the three great Greek injunctions:

a. Man know thyself!

b. Man become the master of thyself!

c. Man seek union with thyself, become thy higher Self!

From the foregoing, therefore, it is clear that the Great Work really deals with the most important and highest task that any mature human being can engage in; that it constitutes the greatest human ideal; and that it deals with the essence of what man has come to earth to accomplish--whence its very appropriate name of Magnum Opus or Great Work.

The chief aim of the Great Work can also be found in the short explanation that Jesus, as all true spiritual Teachers of humanity, has given to his life and work: "I have come that you may have a life more abundant." If there is one thing that is sacred in this world and which can immediately be recognized as such, it is life; for it is life with its essence and all of its attributes that is the most important or "holy thing." If we accept this statement which, to me, is self-evident, then it becomes apparent that man's greatest task is to consciously expand, heighten, and deepen the expression of life, in all its manifestations, both in himself and in others.

To "consciously expand, heighten and deepen the expression of life" implies, first and foremost, to know what life is, to be able to recognize and identify the manyfold manifestations of life within and around oneself, and to be able to experience the manifestation and unfoldment of life in one's being and in one's life. Thus the Great Work necessarily begins with systematic work on oneself, whatever the discipline and tradition used to accomplish this may be and whatever is the label used to describe this work on oneself.

Both in the world and in man, life has three fundamental expressions: the physical, the psychic, and the spiritual. While these three expressions are both qualitatively and quantitatively different from one other, each obeying its own distinctive laws, in essence they are one as life is fundamentally one. This, incidentally, is one of the mysteries and major applications of the Trinity which plays such an important role in the Western Spiritual Tradition. On the physical level, life manifests itself essentially as growth, change, motility; on the psychic planes, as consciousness; and on the spiritual planes, as the source and substance of life or light.

In creation, life descends from the Divine Plane to the physical plane in successive phases of involution that imprison and restrict life in more and more material forms. Having reached its nadir of crystallization in matter, life then begins to reascend the Planes back to its Divine Source and Origin through successive phases of evolution. Here life organizes its manifestation through different vehicles that become more and more differentiated and sensitive as time goes by and which allow for an increasingly more conscious expression of life. Man here can be seen as the most advanced and complex set of vehicles for the expression of life from the physical to the Divine Planes. But man is not yet a finished being; he is an incomplete being undergoing an evolution the aim of which is to perfect and complete his being. Thus, in man, life expresses and unfolds itself essentially as consciousness, and human consciousness is, therefore, the existential essence of man.

The history of man on earth is the biography of the progressive unfoldment of human consciousness from its animal origins to its spiritual destiny. In man, nature becomes conscious of itself and God finds a conscious vehicle of expression in creation. Expressed in the symbols of the Hagia Sophia, life which is "force" in the "Father" and "form" in the "Mother," unfolds as "consciousness" in the "Son." In man, therefore, the study of life is the study of human consciousness, its nature, dynamics, and unfoldment.

The achievement of self-knowledge, therefore, involves the systematic study of human consciousness, its structures and functions, and its conscious and active expansion. The history of human civilization and culture, the countless vicissitudes of man on earth are, at bottom, but an unconscious and conscious way of unfolding his human consciousness, both quantitatively and qualitatively, horizontally and vertically, on one plane of being and through the many planes of being. Traditionally, theology tackled this problem from one angle and science from another angle with philosophy seeking to synthesize the two from its own perspective. Today, however, these basic branches of human knowledge have splintered into the various "natural sciences," "social sciences," an anemic "theology" which has lost most of its erstwhile prestige and authority, and a philosophy that has done all but forsake its traditional synthesizing function for all knowledge.

The need for Illumination (for developing the faculties and abilities necessary for obtaining and synthesizing an integral knowledge of reality, both in its outer and inner aspects) and for Holiness (for developing and unifying, at the conscious level, one's whole being) have remained as constant, perennial, and unfulfilled needs of man, assuming different forms and manifestations at different periods in his history and cultural development. Since the last great "revolution of consciousness and knowledge" which took place during the Enlightenment and its aftermath, the 19th century, and which focused upon a rational-empirical view of reality and synthesis of knowledge, man has sought self-knowledge, self-mastery, and self-actualization evermore desperately but fruitlessly as he proceeded in a direction where these could not be found. From the second half of the 19th century to the end of the first half of the 20th century, however, the sacred traditions of the past surfaced again in various mystical, occult, magical, and spiritual "schools" and "disciplines" characterized by a strongly "esoteric" flavor and orientation. They were clearly counter-cultural and deviant in their basic assumptions and conclusions, and especially in their methods of presentation; thus, they were rejected by the scientific, academic, and theological orthodoxies of our epoch which ridiculed them, surrounded them by a wall of silence or sensationalism, and

dismissed them as heresies and superstitions of the past.
These schools and disciplines, however, contained the
"missing links" and the "synthesis" which our anemic theology
and our ever-splintering sciences had lost and were searching
for in vain in the wrong direction and through inappropriate
methodologies. Culture and counter-culture will eventually
have to be synthesized at a higher level, containing the
essence and best of what is valid for both; this is what I
see happening today and to which I hope to be able to make
some modest contribution.

Religion, philosophy, and science were once unified and
integrated in a harmonious whole which constitutes the true
science and art of the sacred traditions, their central aim
being the production of true sages or Priest-Philosopher-
Kings. Today, the same need and ideal is surfacing again in
the thrust, which is more or less conscious and deliberate in
various thinkers and searchers, to produce a synthesis of the
best of modern human and social science with the valid insights
of the great sacred traditions of the past and to fuse religious
and esoteric disciplines with the methodologies and insights
of modern psychology to generate a higher form of therapy which
will operate as a functional substitute for the Mysteries of
the past. Here, the new sanity and ideal which is now being
envisioned is not only to heal those who are sick and to help
the maladapted person adjust to his social environment and
learn how to "live with himself," but also and especially to
actualize his latent potentialities and faculties, to transcend
himself and thus fulfill his true destiny.

In the past, self-knowledge, self-mastery, and self-
actualization were high and distant goals reserved for the
few who were set apart from the rest of humanity and who were
especially trained for this purpose through rigorous and very
demanding disciplines. Today, however, these great and fundamental aims of human nature are open to all who truly search
for and desire them, and can be realized through methodologies
which are designed to get down to the essentials of the work,
cutting out all the details and the unnecessary ideological
and semantical adornments and incumberances with which they
were clothed and masked in the past. The Quest and its essentials remain the same but its cultural vehicles and expression
must be adapted to our present times and needs. Thus the Great
Work is, once again, reappearing on the contemporary scene,
clothed in modern dress and carried out through a modern approach which answers the needs, ideals, and consciousness of
our epoch.

At the heart of the Great Work, we find certain very simple
universal, and unchanging elements which can be summarized as
follows:

1. A psychospiritual discipline aiming at consciously and
   progressively altering, transforming, and expanding human
   consciousness so as to give birth to a new and qualitatively different type of consciousness--spiritual consciousness.

2. A philosophy of life and an ethic by which to organize and
   structure one's entire daily life so as to progressively
   incarnate and live what was revealed in the higher state
   of consciousness.

   This psychospiritual discipline and way of life are
grounded in the two central axes of all genuine traditions,
i.e. the love of God and the love of man. In the Western
Spiritual Tradition, the specific formulation of these two
main axes is: "Thou shalt love the Lord thy God with all
thy heart, all thy soul, and all thy mind, and thy fellow-
men as thyself." Underpinning the love of God is worship,
climbing the Sacred Mountain wherein the Divine dwells and can
be encountered (i.e. a systematic and effective alteration
and heightening of one's human consciousness in the direction
of the superconscious, its energies, impulses, and life).
Underpinning the love of man is service, helping one's fellow-
men to unfold their being and actualize their potentialities
to the highest extent so that life may express through them
as consciously and as fully as possible. The science (knowledge)
and art (practice) of effective worship and the science and
art of effective service constitute the very center of the
spiritual life which was and is the aim of the sacred traditions.
Moreover, in their almost unanimous teaching, worship must
precede service which completes it as, in order to have the
means to truly help one's fellow-men, one must be illuminated,
vitalized, and guided by the Light of the Spirit. The synthesis and culmination of worship and service is union with
God (or with one's spiritual Self) which has ever been the
final and supreme goal of the sacred traditions.

   The modern social sciences which are now aiming at
developing an integral science of man, an effective art of
living, and a comprehensive philosophy of life with a practical
ethic, are aiming in exactly the same direction but using
a different vocabulary and methodology. Beginning with direct
experience rather than with conceptualized revelation, and
starting with the known and the conscious to thrust towards
the unknown and the superconscious, they are also aiming at
an effective form of worship, psychospiritual development,
and at a practical art of living, or right human relationships.
Under different names and proceeding through different methodologies, the Path and the Quest are one and the same. Thus
in psychosynthesis, for example, which is the most advanced
form and the best synthesis of the modern social sciences, the
Great Work is developed through the following stages:

1. <u>Acquiring systematic knowledge of</u>:

    a. The field of consciousness, the seven functions of the psyche--willing, thinking, feeling, intuition, imagination, biopsychic drives and impulses, and sensations.

    b. The subconscious, the stored memories of one's entire life and the way to get at them and to organize them.

    c. The unconscious, the biopsychic drives, instincts and complexes, and the way to get at them and to integrate them.

    d. The superconscious, the creative spiritual energies and materials of the higher Self and of Its sphere of consciousness, and how to get at them and to integrate them in the psyche.

2. <u>Acquiring mastery of</u>:

    a. The functions of the psyche and their coordination.

    b. The materials of the subconscious.

    c. The energies and materials of the unconscious.

    d. The energies, inspirations, and materials of the super-conscious.

3. <u>Discovering one's human and spiritual Self</u> and aligning one's personality with them.

4. <u>Creating a new and this time consciously fashioned person-ality</u> as the trained vehicle for the human and spiritual Self.

    Beginning with personal psychosynthesis which deals with the systematic exploration and organization of one's own psyche, this approach then leads to interpersonal psycho-synthesis wherein one continues the foregoing by interacting with others and by using one's personality as an organ of interaction, and by discovering one's own "psychological type," the other "psychological types" that exist, and how to mean-ingfully and constructively relate with them. Both stages culminate in self-actualization which consists in the conscious and deliberate development and organization of one's person-ality (psychological work). Self-actualization then leads to the third stage, transpersonal or spiritual psychosynthesis, which consists in discovering and aligning one's human self and personality with the spiritual Self, the Divine Spark within, and which culminates in Self-realization, the offering

of a trained and efficient "temple" or vehicle to the
Spirit for the manifestation of Its attributes in the world.
Without the building of the "Temple of Solomon" (i.e. the
personality, self-actualization), the Light, Fire, and Life
of the Spirit would have no way of becoming conscious of themselves in the world and of manifesting themselves therein.
Without the Quest for God, the discovery of the spiritual
Self, or Self-realization, the most perfectly developed personality would have neither an ultimate purpose nor a true
source of life and being; thus both must work together.

In dealing with an effective science and art of worship,
which is crucial both to the sacred traditions of the past
and to modern psychosynthesis, the creative synthesis of the
spiritual disciplines with the best of modern science has come
up with a very useful and practical scheme: clarify what are
the functions of the psyche which are used, through what processes, and with what results, in the practice of worship,
and train these faculties, gradually and progressively, so
that they can be used effectively. Thus:

1. Willing is used in concentration and affirmation which
    provides energy and focus to the whole operation.

2. Thinking is used in meditation in its threefold stages of
    reflective, receptive, and contemplative meditation. This
    provides knowledge and the focusing of the mind.

3. Feeling is used in adoration or devotion which provides
    energy, emotion, and drive.

4. Imagination is used in visualization, which can become
    vision when fired by the spiritual energies, and provides
    life, focus, and motivation.

5. Intuition is obtained through the creative fusion of as-
    piration operating through invocation and of inspiration
    operating through evocation, or through the synthesis of
    human effort and Divine Grace. From this synthesis results
    an actual breakthrough of the superconscious into the con-
    scious, the dawning of spiritual consciousness, which is the
    central objective of both the sacred traditions and of
    height and transpersonal psychology which are being de-
    veloped today.

6. Biospychic drives, impulses and desires, can and should be
    harnessed and their powerful energies channelled and focused
    through self-mastery and transmutation.

7. Finally, sensations can be developed and amplified through
    careful and precise observation and sensory awareness ex-
    ercises.

The dawning of a new and qualitatively different stage of consciousness, of spiritual consciousness, is the first great goal of all human disciplines which are answering the deepest and truest needs of our age and which provides the foundation for the beginning, as well as the completion, of the Great Work of man, in its universal and perennial form of genuine psychosynthesis, working social integration, and experienced union with God.

CHAPTER III

SPIRITUALITY AND THE SPIRITUAL TRADITION

In the present chapter, I plan to discuss the following questions:

A. What is Spirituality?

B. What is the Spiritual or Primordial Tradition?

C. How I became involved with these "adventures" and how you, too, if you are genuinely interested in and ready for them, can do the same.

A. What is Spirituality?

Briefly put, spirituality is the "fruit" and the ultimate end of all religions, Christian and non-Christian, Western and Eastern, primitive and modern, which they seek to achieve and to foster in their devotees. It is also the evolutionary stage in human development which we can call "maturity" and the state of being and consciousness which all human beings are, consciously or unconsciously, striving to achieve--it is the goal of human evolution and the destiny of man towards which all human experiences and all human endeavors are leading. Spirituality, moreover, is essentially a state of human consciousness--a certain way of thinking, feeling, and willing which profoundly affects our way and style of living and, therefore, our being: what we are and what we become. As such, it is not synonymous with religion even though it is intimately connected with it; the ultimate purpose of religion, in fact, is to unfold spirituality in its followers.

Religion, in general, provides us both with a partial representation, or image of spirituality, and with a set of teachings and principles by which man, after long and arduous efforts, will someday be able to achieve and realize spirituality. A "picture," however, is not to be confused with the reality for which it stands. In the world, one may meet many athletes who are not training to become such, and one may find people in gymnasiums who are training themselves, but who are very far from being athletes. Similarly, religion should not be confused with spirituality which is its aim and ideal. Moreover, religions are many while spirituality is, essentially, one; reality and truth are one, but there are many conceptual schemes

21

to represent their various facets, aspects, and dimensions, just as there are many approaches and paths that lead to them. Religions utilize different symbol systems, different conceptual schemes, and different approaches, which are best suited to the people they serve, to lead them to the unfold-ment and realization of their own spirituality. As such, religions are mainly culture bound, relative, partial, and unfolding. Spirituality, on the other hand, being based upon a direct personal experience and realization of reality, is trans cultural and truly universal, though expressing itself through many phases, degrees, and levels of realization.

What is being generally viewed today as a "religious crisis," I see essentially as being a "spiritual crisis." At the root of this crisis stands the unfortunate fact that, by and large, established religions are unable to show forth in their leaders and exponents examples of genuine and living spirituality. They fail to make their symbols and teachings meaningful, relevant, and practical for their followers and, therefore, they are unable to foster and develop genuine spirituality in their members. Unfortunately, there are not too many Saints and Mystics to go around!

The answer to that crisis I see as being essentially "spiritual" rather than "religious," i.e. to find or educate people who possess some degree of genuine spirituality, who will be drawn to official religion, and who will be capable of interpreting in modern, meaningful, and practical terms the traditional symbols and teachings of religion and of of-fering a living example of what a modern spiritual person can be.

Though spirituality is essentially a personal experience, a state of consciousness or awareness, which must be achieved and personaly experienced by an individual to be truly under-stood in its depths, certain of its general features and basic characteristics can be outlined intellectually. These are the following:

1. The general expression of spirituality.

2. The specific expression of spirituality.

3. The distinguishing features of spirituality.

1. The general expression of spirituality.

At the general level, spirituality is the direct result and indicator of man's overall "maturity," or evolutionary status, on several levels. It is a cardinal assumption of the Spiritual Tradition, which was taught openly by the Ancient Sages and by many religions, that

man is composed of four "elements" and, therefore, that
he undergoes a fourfold development or evolution. These
four "elements" were represented by the symbols of Earth,
Water, Air, and Fire which represent, respectively, the
physical, emotional, mental, and spiritual dimensions of
man's being and human consciousness. Man's fourfold evolution, or maturation process, can, therefore, be traced
and evaluated in terms of his "four ages": his physical
age, his emotional age, his mental age, and his spiritual
age. His physical age is easily discerned by the number
of chronological years that have elapsed since birth. His
emotional age can be determined, in a somewhat more com-
plicated fashion, by his capacity for feeling, for empathy
and sympathy, as well as by what he is emotionally drawn
to and is attracting to himself. His mental age depends
on his capacity for thinking and reasoning, on his mental
perceptiveness and alertness, on his ability to reason, to
analyze, and to synthesize in a clear, cogent, and integrated fashion the various data and experiences which his
attention has selected. Finally, his spiritual age depends
on the degree of spiritual consciousness which he has unfolded and on his capacity to grasp intuitively and to
harmonize with the creative Source and Essence of his being,
with the creative energies feeding and vitalizing his
capacity to know, to love, and to create: to understand
what he is, whence he came, whither he goes, and what is
the purpose of this life on earth and the specific and
concrete functions of his everyday experiences.

In its general expression, spirituality implies a
certain amount of emotional, mental, and spiritual maturity,
though not necessarily a certain physical age, such that
spiritual consciousness--the awareness of one's Divine
Spark and of Its Will and Attributes--may freely and consciously express themselves through man's aspirations,
thoughts, feelings, and will, and manifest in his life
and behavior. Here, spirituality implies that man's soul
and its temporary dwelling place, the body, have become
well-developed and coordinated vehicles and finely tuned
instruments for the expression and manifestation, at the
conscious level in this world, of man's spiritual nature
and aspirations. As such, the spiritual man becomes a
natural "leader" in whatever line of endeavor he gets involved with. From the outside, empirically, he can be
observed to be highly vital, intelligent, and a very successful
person. The functioning of his higher state of spiritual
consciousness, operating through well-coordinated mental
and emotional vehicles and, possibly, through an equally
well developed, strong, and healthy body, gives him a
distinct advantage in the struggle for survival and for
self-affirmation in his everyday life.

Whatever situation in life a person who has developed a general level of spirituality may find himself in, whatever occupation, sport, or line of endeavor he may engage in, he is sure to succeed in it and to distinguish himself therewith, in a manner that is plainly visible and ascertainable in the most practical and empirical way. Having a "passion for excellence," being committed to fulfill whatever task he finds himself involved in to the utmost of his human capacity, perceiving a deeper meaning and purpose behind all the seemingly trivial vicissitudes of everyday life, and dedicating all his actions and undertaking not to "success" or to "a human person," or even to his sense of self-affirmation, but to the birth and unfoldment of the God within, and being vitalized and dynamized, in his aspirations, thoughts, feelings, and will by spiritual energies, the spiritual man cannot avoid distinguishing himself and standing out as an "unusual, highly vital, creative, resourceful, and capable person."

However, the empirical expressions or external manifestations of spirituality--inspiration, creative thinking, vital energies, resourcefulness, and success--do not represent and describe the heart and core of spirituality which is qualitatively different and which lies on a different plane. This plane is not the behavioral or empirical plane but, rather, the plane of human consciousness or of inward realization. It is within the depths of the human psyche, in a purified and sanctified heart and mind alone, that the essence and the true secrets of spirituality are revealed and experienced through a tremendous and qualitative expansion of man's capacity to know and to understand, to love and to feel, to create and to will, and not in his external behavior or achievements. Thus, to the unenlightened and inwardly unawakened person, spirituality is destined to remain an eternal mystery and enigma. . . until it will dawn and express itself within the core of his own inner being. Strength, success, resourcefulness, and leadership are not by themselves indicators of spiritual realization and spiritual maturity as many concrete and historical examples have readily shown.

2. The specific expression of spirituality.

In contradistinction with the former, the specific expression of spirituality, which is an earlier phase or developmental stage of it, does not require a general and coordinated "maturity" or development of man's emotional, mental, and spiritual "ages" and "dimensions." What it does demand and that which is its distinctive feature, is the breakthrough and emergence of spiritual consciousness.

Thus a person may have achieved only a slight degree of emotional or mental development and still have experienced a genuine expression of spiritual consciousness, as witnessed by Saints, Seers, and religious leaders who were far from being emotional or mental giants, and who were certainly not "balanced" in their emotional, mental, and spiritual manifestations. That degree of balance, or proper coordination and harmonization of all of man's faculties around his spiritual consciousness, is characteristic of the more advanced stage of general spirituality. As it is quite apparent, man can be highly trained at the physical level (e.g. the athlete) without being equally developed at the emotional and mental levels; or he can be highly emotionally developed and sensitive (e.g. the artist) without being physically or mentally trained; finally, he can be highly mentally trained (e.g. the intellectual)without being physically or emotionally developed. The same, therefore, is also true for the spiritual dimension and for spiritual consciousness which can express itself without necessarily requiring a high level of physical, emotional, and mental development and coordination. Man does not evolve at an even and harmonious pace and may show quite a discrepancy in his four "ages."

In his manifestation of the Divine Light, each person may show certain emphases and weak points. Spiritual Light is the source and essence of knowledge, love, and power; man, through different personal experiences and varying emphases on different psychospiritual centers, may manifest, both subjectively and objectively, different emphases upon knowledge, love, and power. Thus, in unfolding spirituality, one may temporarily travel along the Path of Knowledge (the Occultist), the Path of Love (the Mystic), or the Path of Power (the Magician or Practical Occultist). At the higher levels of spiritual maturity, however, these must be properly fused and integrated, just as man's four "ages" must be balanced and integrated to become "awakened" and refined "instruments" of the Divine Spark which has now indrawn into the human psyche and which is consciously expressing Its Will and Attributes.

3. The distinguishing features of spirituality.

What are the major distinguishing features of spiritual consciousness which are sui generis and qualitatively different from those of emotional and mental consciousness? To begin with these constitute an inner, direct, experiential realization of the individual in whom spiritual consciousness is blooming and they carry with them a certainty, reality, and depth of experience

that no external or intellectual teachings could ever
impart. Briefly put, these are:

a. The deep experience and inner realization that one's
    true self, the creative and living Source and Essence
    of one's being, which it is our destiny and task to
    consciously identify or "unite with," is neither phys-
    ical, psychic or psychosocial but, rather, spiritual,
    in its nature. And that, as such, it is an immortal
    and integral part or "Spark" of the Cosmic Spirit
    which can never be destroyed or annihilated by any
    human experience and which must eventually reach its
    intended destiny: the conscious realization of its
    perfection.

b. The deep experience and inner realization that life on
    earth is good and infinitely valuable, that it is a
    great gift and a priceless opportunity for man to un-
    fold all of his human powers and faculties and to be-
    come his true Self: a conscious, individualized
    creator; that this world was created by God, who is
    man's Father, as well as Love, Wisdom, and Creative
    Energy, and that this world is ruled, up to its
    smallest and most "insignificant" details by Divine
    Providence; that, ultimately, Divine Justice does
    prevail and that all human experiences have a purpose,
    a reason, and a meaning which are "just and good":
    that there is absolutely no human experience, bar none,
    from which man cannot learn and benefit, provided he
    approaches them in the proper frame of mind, that is
    through spiritual consciousness and as a gift of God
    which, in fact, it is!

c. The deep experience and inner realization that incar-
    nation in this world and all human experiences therein
    are, ultimately, "means" or "lessons" by which man can
    find and unite with the God within or the "unknown
    greater Self" and, therefore, that all human activities
    and events should be dedicated to the Great Quest
    for God and the Great Work for a life more conscious,
    more full, and more abundant. It is also the inner
    realization that the final "yardstick" or evaluative
    criterion for all human experiences and undertakings
    is not whether these are "pleasant" or "unpleasant,"
    "successful" or "unsuccessful" but, rather, whether
    they are helping or hindering, retarding or accel-
    erating, the birth and unfoldment of the Christ within,
    the dawning of genuine spiritual consciousness.

d. Finally, the specific and concrete realization and
    understanding of the daily tasks and lessons which

the given person has come into incarnation to accomplish and a consecration of one's self, time, and
resources to accomplish the "mission" or set of tasks
one has come to carry out as fully as it is humanly
possible.

B.   What is the Spiritual or Primordial Tradition?

Unlike other human traditions such as the scientific,
the philosophical, or even the theological which organize and
articulate themselves in schools or societies and whose major
assumptions, teachings, and philosophies are objectified and
systematized in books and social institutions, the Spiritual
Tradition is embodied and transmitted by living human beings
who are generally not organized in formal institutions. It
is expressed in the conscious experience and personal realization, in the soul, or psyche, of those who have attained
a given level of spiritual consciousness or "specific spirituality."

The Spiritual or Primordial Tradition is completely
universal and stretches all the way back to the dawn of human
thinking and of human evolution; it is a living, dynamic, and
unfolding vision and realization of human consciousness in
which the spiritual level has become active in men and women of
all races, religions, and social strata. As such, it is a
transcultural and non-institutionalized realization of the
"Essence of Reality"--of God, man, and nature, and of their
relationship and destiny--which certain human beings have
achieved and which, ultimately, all human beings will achieve.
Its fundamental pre-requisites are a certain "spiritual age"
and "level of human consciousness and development" which, when
achieved, admits a given human being into the great human
spiritual brotherhood which exists on both sides of the grave,
in this world where it must be earned, and in the next, where
it endures and is acknowledged.

Resting upon an inner revelation and realization which
can only be personally experienced and which is a living,
unfolding, and on-going process, its essence can never be expressed in books and dogmas and its members, or adepts, cannot
be organized into a "school" or "institution." True, many
fragments, symbols, and analogical representations of its
basic "tenets" and "realizations" have been codified and objectified in various books, teachings, and thought systems,
but its essence and living fundamentals which must, by their
very nature, remain a personal achievement and a personal experience,have not. These partial fragments, images, and analogical representations have been organized and given to the
world by three major sources:

1. The World Religions, which draw their very life and essence from them.

2. The Mystery Schools, which seek to train and qualify worthy and ready aspirants to its realizations and "membership."

3. Individual Seers, Prophets, Poets, and Sages who have found literary, artistic, or philosophic media to convey their experiences and realizations of spiritual consciousness to other human beings, holding up before them a great ideal and a great promise which they, too, shall someday be able to realize.

The basic tenets and philosophy of the Spiritual Tradition, being rooted in a personal and direct experience and realization, can never be learned ab extra from sermons, lectures, books, or essays, but only ab intra through the revelations and hierophanies of one's own Divine Spark. Priests, Saints, Sages, and Initiates, who have themselves achieved a certain degree of spiritual awakening and of spiritual consciousness, enter the "living stream" of the Primordial Tradition but they cannot impart these treasures to their followers, devotees, and loved ones; at best, they can only "prepare the way for Him who is to come"--for the Christ within, the Divine Spark, Who is the Great and only Hierophant of the Spiritual Mysteries.

Thus a young child in Tibet, an old woman in India, a businessman in America, a prisoner in Russia, a shepherd in China, and a fisherman in France, for example, may be linked with the Spiritual Tradition and become its carrier and living representative when genuine spiritual consciousness has begun to dawn in their psyche and illumines their lives and beings, even if they have never heard the word before and if they never went to any school, church, or "Temple of the Mysteries," for they will have become "Initiates of its Mysteries" which is the only "badge of admission" which such a tradition has. Were they to meet in the world, they would be able to recognize and to understand each other better than a mother or father understands his child, or the master his pupil, and the priest his faithful. This is because they have experienced the same reality and communed with the same Spirit which has revealed Its Mysteries to them, and not because they have attended the "same school." Moreover, they would instantly recognize each other by certain signs which their spiritual vision would reveal to them, which can never be faked, and which tell each their respective rank and status in the spiritual brotherhood of humanity.

The Spiritual or Primordial Tradition, therefore, is not an outer school or organization, but an inner achievement and

realization; it is not based upon a particular teaching or
book, but upon certain specific experiences and developments
of human consciousness; it is not bound by race, time, or
place, but it stretches out to embrace the whole of humanity
in a living, growing, unfolding synthesis of spiritual consciousness; it can never be taught or conferred ab extra,
but only obtained by one's efforts, achievements, and maturity ab intra. Rather than being a group of people discussing certain tenets, teachings, or books of the "Masters,"
it is a brotherhood of personal experience and existential
realization or "Initiation." Its members have not gone to
the "same school" or joined the "same society," and thus they
are not unified by its "classics" or by its "constitution,"
rather, they are more like a club of alpinists or explorers
who have climbed the same mountains and explored the same
country even if by different paths and in different degrees.

It is not words, ideas, or principles shared in common
that unites them and enables them to communicate with and
understand each other, but a shared set of experiences, the
partaking of the same reality and communing with the same
spirit. This fact raises an interesting problem and points
to a cardinal teaching of the Spiritual Tradition, namely,
that truth, unity, reality, brotherhood, and a genuine cognitive synthesis of reality and of all human experience
(which is the most profound, vital, and ambitious of all
undertakings of human knowledge), together with the solution
of the most fundamental problems of humanity--the riddle of
the Sphinx, the Mystery of Life, and the enigma of the Universe--
cannot be realized and attained by the "natural man," but only
by the "spiritual man"; that the most vital, ultimate, and important questions of human knowledge and human curiosity cannot
be contained or satisfied by science, philosophy, or theology,
which operate mainly ab extra through the intellectual dimension, but only by a personal spiritual awakening and an
initiation into spiritual consciousness, by the "Spiritual
Tradition" living in the heart and soul of the purified and
regenerated human being. This is another reason why it has
been said: "Seek ye first the Kingdom of Heaven (i.e. spiritual consciousness) and all of these things shall be added
unto you" and "the wisdom of the world (i.e. natural consciousness) is foolishness (i.e. incomplete and lacking its
essence) in the eyes of God (i.e. of the spiritually illuminated and awakened consciousness). Who can reveal His
Mysteries in the heart of a child"(i.e. in the consciousness
of one who though young in biological years is old in spiritual
maturity).

C. How I became involved with these "adventures" and how
    you, too, if you are genuinely interested in and ready
    for them, can do the same.

        As a child, and even more acutely and intensely so as
an adolescent, I was a very restless, dissatisfied, and lonely
person with powerful energies and drives flowing through my
being which neither my parents nor I could really understand
and cope with adequately. The answers to the endless questions
about myself and why I was the way I was, about life, and about
the "why of things" which I got from my parents, teachers, and
clergy did not satisfy me and did not "fit in" with my own
personal experiences and with the realizations of my inner
consciousness. Something undefined, yet most important, was
missing, something which could best be described as a "yearning
for substance and reality, for completeness and synthesis"
was lacking. This undefined hunger, this profound dissatis-
faction with the world-views and basic answers I was given,
this "inner substantial poverty" was the motivating spring
which launched me on a "metaphysical quest" for Truth, for
Being, and for a life more full, abundant, and consciously
lived. After voracious readings and interminable discussions
with a wide variety of people, and long travels in many countries
spiced with many experiences, I soon came to the conclusion
that science, philosophy, and religion, such as I could find
them in modern institutions and in key sources which they
provided, did not have the answers I was seeking and could not
satisfy my deep inner hunger for knowing and understanding.
At this point, I vowed to myself that I would spend most of my
life and resources to find these answers wherever they could
be found and under whatever labels or symbols they might be
couched, and to articulate them and develop them for myself,
if I could not "find them" in the world. After a long and
rather "dry period," punctuated by more traveling and experiences, I came across certain books on Eastern Yoga and, later,
on world mysticism, which set my heart on fire and my mind in
a state of great ferment. Here, at last, in black and white
and in well articulated sentences, I found a correspondence
and conceptualization of the deepest truths and insights I had
earlier found within the recesses of my own psyche. This
proved to me that I was not alone in this quest and that other,
well-known and respected human beings, had experienced, even
to a greater extent, what I had experienced or intuited vaguely
but compellingly. Thus, I set upon a new program of study and
went about collecting as many such books as I could find in
Paris, London, and New York. After a while, I became satiated
with books and longed to meet the human beings who had written
these books, who had lived and personally experienced these
things, and who could, therefore, guide me and advise me on my
quest.

After an extended and fruitless search, characterized
by many disappointments and "crashing pedestals," when I least
expected it, but most needed it, I met the first genuine mystic
and, through her, three or four others. Recognizing a profound kinship with such people and also that they knew and
had realized far more than I, I set upon seeking to unfold
within myself what I recognized and admired in them. Their
most unanimous and persistent warning, however, was that
they could not "teach me" or "give me" what I hungered for,
but merely "point the way" to what I should do to unfold
spiritual consciousness in myself.

After many years of absorbing reading and much experimentation, and of many, many experiences of all kinds, I
finally began to realize that the "answers" to the "riddles"
and "mysteries" I sought could only come from within myself
through a personally lived experience and realization and not
from the outside, from books, words, or lectures. Then, as
some of these "mysteries" and "riddles" began to unveil their
deeper meanings and implications, I marveled at the greatness,
wisdom, and love of God, at the beauty and preciousness of
life, at the great opportunities which "knock at the door of
our consciousness" everyday. I marveled at the Divine Justice
which underpins all human events and experiences and I embarked
upon one of the most fascinating, stimulating, and life-giving
of all human experiences--the spiritual adventure. I also
realized experientially the truth of the old saying of Angelus
Silesius: "If that which thou seekest thou findest not within
thyself, thou wilt surely not find it without."

If some of you are also genuinely discontented by the
explanations of the fundamental questions of human life given
by the universities and churches, and if you feel drawn to the
spiritual quest as a way to obtaining these answers, I would
say the following things:

1. The first step and the fundamental pre-requisite for the
spiritual adventure is to have a genuine "divine discontentment,"
to feel deeply "to be poor in spirit," i.e. to lack something
which is vitally important to oneself. For this "discontentment" and "hunger" alone will provide the motivational drive
which must sustain one throughout his spiritual quest. Unless
one is genuinely discontented, not because of failure but because of a "substantial emptiness" with the existing thought-
systems (religious, philosophical, and scientific) and with
one's present life, one is not yet ready for the spiritual
adventure.

2. Books, lectures, and discussions (and the concretizing of one's thoughts in essays), though an important step in the process of spiritual development, are not its foundation, not its efficient cause--which is human experience approached in a certain frame of mind (being wholly dedicated to the spiritual quest and to spiritual development). It is also and especially the daily practice of spiritual exercises, to awaken one's spiritual centers and to expand one's conscious-ness, and the living of the "spiritual life."

3. "Spiritual teachers," "mentors," or "guides" are also an important and indispensable element or phase of spiritual de-velopment but, again, they are not its central source. They can only "point the way" and "show the necessary means" to its realization but they cannot tread the Path or do the work which only the individual can do for himself. They are not the spiritual Initiators but they can prepare "the way" for the One who will initiate man into the spiritual Mysteries, for the Divine Spark or Christ-within.

4. While many "secret schools," "mystical brotherhoods," "occult organizations," and "esoteric self-realization methods" do exist and generally have some genuine contribution to make-- if they are legitimate and not "crank groups"--it is the organized World Religions and the teachings and symbols of the well-organized churches which are still the "safest" and the most comprehensive and legitimate channels available for man's spiritual development.

5. Finally, the most important training must begin with one-self, with one's character and personality in one's daily life. For it is only when a genuine "glowing center of attraction," or charisma, has been developed in one's soul, that the true "spiritual adventure" will begin in earnest. For then, and only then, will man consciously draw to himself all the books, all the people, and all the human conditions and experiences he needs for his spiritual development. When a person is gen-uinely ready for the "spiritual quest," no matter where that person might live in the world and no matter what is his con-dition and station in life, he will be provided with all he needs to do so by the Higher Powers. Conversely, should one not be ready for it, no amount of reading, money, or erudition will ever open the "Door to the Spiritual Temple" and "unfasten the gates of spiritual consciousness." Thus, the primary and beginning task of all those who are truly interested in the "spiritual quest" is to become ready.

CHAPTER IV

THE SEVEN FUNDAMENTALS AND THE PRIMORDIAL TRADITION

One of the central problems which all religions, and
world-religions in particular, must face is that of their val-
idity and universality. To whom are the teachings and symbols
of a given religion applicable? What is the relationship
of this religion to other religions? How are its basic dogmas,
creed, and rituals to be viewed--as a set of universal truths
and divine revelations valid for all human beings in all historical periods or as a set of sociocultural products, valid
only for certain people at a certain point of their historical
development? Is there a common core and a common source for
man's various religious approaches and churches? These are
some of the basic questions and problems inherent to and
raised by all great religions which we shall examine in this
chapter.

Interestingly enough, all great world-religions have,
more or less explicitly stated in their pantheon and theology,
a monotheistic conception of God, the conception of One God,
the "Father of the Gods" or of an "Unknown God." It is from
this conception that arose the universal notion of the "Fatherhood of God" and of the "Brotherhood of men," i.e. that all
men come from the same source eventually to return to it and,
therefore, that they are, indeed, "spiritual and human brothers."
This monotheistic conception, moreover, implies that the
Supreme Reality, both within and without man, is One, and that
human beings may have access to that One Reality wherein the
true and final basis for human understanding, human sympathy,
and human cooperation is to be found. As one spiritual school
tersely put it: "we affirm that the mortal may attain to the
knowledge of the spiritual while yet incarnate."[1]

If God, however, the Supreme Reality, the Source and
Essence of all there is and the destiny of man is One, the
symbolic descriptions, the intellectual representations of
the paths, techniques, and ethics which lead thereto are many.
As an old Vedic Text puts it: "God is One but men call Him
by many names." The forms and the interpretations of divine
revelation, of the breakthrough of the superconscious into the
conscious, are, likewise, many. As the great German Mystic
Karl von Eckartshausen writes:

33

"But, when men multiplied, the frailty of man and his
weakness necessitated an exterior society which veiled
the interior one, and concealed the spirit and the truth
in the letter. The people at large were not capable
of comprehending high interior truth, and the danger
would have been too great in confiding that which was
of all most holy to incapable people. Therefore, inward truths were wrapped in external and visible ceremonies, so that men, by the perception of the outer, which
is the symbol of the interior, might by degree be enabled
to safely approach the interior spiritual truths."[2]

Thus not only are there many religons and many theologies
with different symbol systems, metaphysical systems, and
ethical systems, but even within the same religion there are
many "denominations," "splinters," and different interpretations
of the same source of revelation. This is, on the one hand,
because God, the Spirit, does not "speak" directly and con-
ceptually to men and, on the other hand, because men, even
great and inspired men, Prophets and Mystics, receive divine
revelation in accordance with their receptivity for it and
translate it and interpret it in terms of their own level of
consciousness, background of experience, and general understanding
of man and life. Thus revelations and theophanies are always
differentially received and interpreted and, therefore, colored
by the vehicle, human consciousness, through which they manifest.
This process, furthermore, goes through two basic phases: first,
we have the coloring and the interpretation of this revelation by the receptivity and level of human consciousness of
its vehicle, the Prophet or Mystic. Secondly, we have the
different understanding, interpretation, and systematization
of the revelation and experiences of the Prophet or Mystic
by his followers and apologists.

Behind the various theoretical interpretations and ra-
tionalizations of a given religion's revelation and, in fact,
behind the revelation of all religions, stands a fundamental
core of truths, principles, and insights which are, indeed,
one, universal, and valid for all men of all times and places.
As Karl von Eckartshausen writes:

"Meanwhile, a more advanced school has always existed
to which the deposition of all science has been confided, and this school was the community illuminated
interiorly by the Saviour, the society of the Elect, which
has continued from the first day of creation to the
present times; its members, it is true, are scattered
all over the world, but they have always been united
by one spirit and one truth; they have had but one
knowledge, a single source of truth, one lord, one
doctor, and one master, in whom resides substantially
the whole plenitude of God, who also alone initiates
them into the high mysteries of Nature and of the Spiritual World. . ."

This community of light has existed since the first
day of the world's creation, and its duration will
be to the end of time. It is the society of those
elect who know the Light in the Darkness and separate
what is pure therein. This community possesses a
school in which all who thirst for knowledge are in-
structed by the Spirit of Wisdom itself; and all the
mysteries of God and of nature are preserved therein for
the children of light. Perfect knowledge of God, of
of nature, and of humanity are the objects of in-
struction in this school. It is thence that all truths
penetrate into the world; herein is the School of the
Prophets and of all who search for wisdom; it is in
this community alone that truth and the explanation of
all mystery is to be found. It is the most hidden of
communities, yet it possesses members gathered from
nay orders. . . .From all time, therefore, there has
been a hidden assembly, a society of the Elect, of those
who sought for and had a capacity for Light, and this
interior society was called the interior Sanctuary or
Church. All that the external Church possesses in
symbol, ceremony or rite is the letter which expresses
externally the spirit and the truth residing in the
interior Sanctuary. . .
The wisdom of the temple under the ancient alliance was
preserved by priests and by prophets. To the priests
was confided the external, the cortex of hieroglyph.
The prophets had the charge of the inner truth, and their
occupation was continually to recall the priests from the
letter to the spirit when they began to forget the spirit
and cleave only to the letter. The science of the priests
was that of the knowledge of exterior symbols. That of
the prophets was experimental possession of the truth of
the symbols. In the external was the letter; in the interior the spirit lived. There was, therefore, in the
ancient alliance a school of prophets and of priests,
the one occupying itself with the spirit in the emblem,
the other with the emblem itself. . . .
The external Church of the ancient alliance was visible;
the interior Church was always invisible, must be invisible, and yet must govern all, because force and power
are alone confided to her."[3]

The spirit and heart behind the symbols and teachings of
all religions has been known by many names and many labels.
The best known of these are: the "Philosophia Perennis," the
"Haghia Sophia," the "Primordial Tradition," and the"Spiritual
and Mystical Tradition." This core of universal principles and
truths, moreover, is not static and fixed once and for all, but
dynamic and unfolding; it continually grows and expands on its
foundation, not denying it but rendering it fuller and more

complete. The key problem, to get at this universal core behind all religions is to be able to discern and to separate the elements and dimensions which are man-made and, therefore, culture-bound, relating to time and place, and level of evolution, from those which are truly universal, spiritual, and absolute. And, as the sacred texts of humanity and every religion tell us, this is not a matter of erudition or of the study of texts and commentaries, it is a question of expanding one's level of consciousness; for it is not natural reason and scholarship that can reveal these hidden truths but only the Spirit of God, the superconscious. All of the fundamental documents, prayers, and rituals of the world religions do contain both elements which are intermingled together and which coexist simultaneously at different levels--the spiritual and the human, the absolute and the relative.

Analytically speaking, there are 3 major approaches one can take to religion: the emotional or existential, the intellectual or theoretical, and the spiritual or esoteric. The first approach, the emotional or existential, consists basically in joining a given religion, in participating in its community life and in seeking to implement its ethical system and its practical teachings as much as it is humanly and personally possible. The second approach, the intellectual or theoretical one, consists not in becoming a member of this or that religion, but in studying and analyzing systematically its "sacred book," commentaries, and practical teachings in the light of natural reason and in comparison with other religions. Rather than the approach of the faithful or of the devotee, it is the approach of the intellectual and of the professor. The third approach, the spiritual or esoteric one, is that of the Initiate who is capable of deciphering its key symbols, of lifting, at least partially, the veil of its mysteries, and of experiencing in his own being and life, some of its great treasures and promises.

It is also interesting to note how the first and the second approaches deal essentially with the world of multiplicity, with the dimension of the many clashing and opposed religions and denominations, while the third deals essentially with the world of unity, with the dimension of the one living stream of spirituality. Thus it is priests, theologians, and fanatic "true believers" who fight about religion and who seek to promulgate their own religion as the "One True Religion" as against all the other "false" religions. True Mystics and Initiates of the Spiritual Tradition, on the other hand, look beyond the image of the symbols and the analogical garments of a particular form of revelation to its inner core and living foundation in reality which is indeed one.

Most great Western Religions have always claimed that they are universally valid and that they are the "One true Religion." According to the level at which this claim is interpreted, it is both true and false. There is, indeed, a common universal core to these religions which is universally valid, and there is, indeed, "One, Holy, Catholic Church," which is the trunk or source-root whence all religions have drawn their mystical core. This core, as Eckartshausen tells us, has existed since the first day of the world's creation, and its duration will be to the end of time, until all human beings have been spiritually regenerated and have found a conscious and full union with God. This Inner Church has inspired and guided all world religions, providing them with their central mystical core and with their great symbolic blue-prints, but it has never been and will never be fully incarnated and institutionalized on earth.

Let us now turn to true spiritual work, to this mystical core, as it is represented, in a symbolic and veiled fashion, by all religions and in a more direct and rational fashion by the Mystery Schools. The central aim of spiritual development and of spiritual growth, in fact, of life on earth, is to lead man to consciously achieve a fuller being and to live a fuller life. Their ultimate aim is to lead man, by degrees, to become actually, in the here and now of his earthly life, what he is potentially: a spiritual being, a Son of God.

At the practical level, spiritual training and growth have two central objectives, both for one self and for others. These are: illumination and healing. Both involve becoming evermore aware of the Light, and suffusing oneself (i.e. one's Aura and Tree of Life) with the spiritual Light which will then transform us into new beings, spiritual beings. Both are intimately related to each other as illumination implies raising one's consciousness and one's life to higher, more real and vital levels, and as healing implies making the sick well again so that they might then grow towards greater heights of consciousness and levels of being.

Worship, Prayer in its ritualistic or theurgic part, is anchored upon 7 major documents or blue-prints in the Western Spiritual Tradition which have their equivalents or correspondences in the Eastern Tradition or in any genuine Spiritual Tradition for that matter. In these documents, one can find, if one searches deeply enough, when one is mature for this, and when these blue-prints reveal their inner treasures, all the basic knowledge of God, man, and nature, and their relationship to one another. One can also find in them all the symbols needed for concentration, meditation, and contemplation, and all the practical exercises which are necessary to achieve genuine spiritual consciousness and the Birth of the Christ-within. These, therefore, constitute the very heart and substance of the Western Spiritual Tradition and

contain enough information and practical exercises to lead
any human being from the state of nature to the state of
grace, i.e. from a human to a spiritual state. These seven
great documents or fundamentals are:

1. Divine Names.

2. The Sign of the Cross.

3. The Lord's Prayer.

4. The Nicene Creed.

5. The Beatitudes.

6. The Hail Mary.

7. The Ten Commandments.

Each of these documents and glyphs is an autonomous unit and
it is complemented, reinforced, and completed by the others.
Each contains briefly, in the inner structure of its symbols
and relationships:

a. A simple and practical system of spiritual development and
    of self-realization.

b. A cognitive system containing a philosophy of man, of his
    being, origin, and destiny.

c. An integrated set of psychospiritual exercises designed
    to awaken and activate certain Centers on the Tree of Life,
    to open up certain "doors" and "layers" of consciousness,
    and to stimulate certain energies into activity--to alter
    and expand human consciousness and to lead to the dawning
    of genuine spiritual consciousness through a progressive
    purification, consecration, and illumination of man's
    Tree of Life and Aura.

d. A blue-print for formulating and realizing ideals, the
    art of thought-form creation, projection, and realization.

CHAPTER V

DIVINE NAMES: THEIR NATURE AND USE

From time immemorial there has been known to all advanced students of the Mysteries, to Prophets, Mystics, and Initiates of all races and ages, an arcane Art and Science based on the use of Names of Power. This Art and Science of self-actualization and spiritual Initiation has been called by many names and has assumed many forms and expressions. In the East, it is best known under the name of Mantra Yoga while in the West it is called Theurgy by the Occult Schools and The Way of the Name by Mystic Schools. This method of using Names of Power is most important for anyone who is seriously interested in spiritual work and who is ready for it; this because it constitutes the first and most important pillar of all true spiritual science, whether of the East or of the West, in the Lesser or in the Greater Mysteries, on the Occult Path as well as on the Mystical Path. This method, moreover, will be used by the aspirant to the Mysteries from his first entry on the Path, where he shall find it at its very "door," as it were, all the way through his final achievement of Christhood or Spiritual Illumination. As such, it is an absolutely vital part of all true spiritual training for the Neophyte as well as for the full Adept. Finally, it is also the first and most important of the seven keys to full spiritual growth and Initiation.

The use of Names of Power is an Art as well as a Science for it contains general theoretical principles which are true for all men and practical applications which yield results that are both universal, at one level, and unique to the practitioner, at another. As a science, this method can be described and formalized in a theoretical scheme but, as an art, it can only be personally lived and experienced.

Why are names so important for man, not only in the psychic and spiritual fields, but also in everyday life? Because the capacity to name things implies, among other things, the power of reason, a language, human consciousness, which are man's distinctive traits as a human being. This capacity has been with us from the very beginning of man's evolution on earth and will remain with us until the end of our evolution here. Already in Genesis, we find God telling man to give a name to all the creatures of the air, sea, and earth, and to all the objects of creation. And we find, again and again, in all sacred Scriptures, a very strong value being put upon God revealing His Name to His servants. The religious importance of God's Name was so great that there is even one of the Ten Commandments which urges men not to "take the Name of the Lord God in vain." The Lord's Prayer, which is another important key to spiritual training in the West, also contains one special petition or formula: "Hallowed be Thy Name." Finally, one of the external clues by which one can discern a true student of the Mysteries is that he will never use lightly or irreverently any Divine Name for he knows, by his own personal experience, their power and holiness.

In our present civilization we can readily see how important it is to name a child when he is born and to know the name (and the address) of a person we would like to get in touch with. The naming and "labelling" of people and of things is of such importance that science is constantly coining new names for what it discovers. Furthermore, to know someone or something, we must know his name. Without names there would be no language and no systematic knowledge of anything; and without language there would be no reason and no human consciousness, and without these there would be no human beings. Conversely, looking towards the future, we could say that without knowing and using Divine Names man would find it difficult to know God and to continue his human evolution towards spiritual evolution and to achieve his eventual union with God.

It is simple to see why names are so important for man. They are symbols, psychic media, which convey and elicit the various units of human consciousness which we call intuitions, thoughts, feelings, and vital energies. They are true "units" of human consciousness, "streams of focused ideas and emotions," and "bundles of energy." They are the lens which direct and focus our whole attention upon one aspect of reality, upon one power or being. They function as catalysts which awaken, which invoke and evoke, certain energies and states of consciousness in our psyche. In short, they are psychospiritual means by which we invoke a certain Presence, induce a certain state of consciousness, and focus our awareness; by which we recreate in ourselves an "image" or "facsimile" of that which is without or above us. Names are so important to man, in all his activities, sacred and profane, because they are the means by which man deliberately awakens and focuses his intuitions, thoughts, feelings, and energies by an effort of the will. Names, therefore, are the key regulators and switches of man's human consciousness and of his inner life. It is through Names (words, images, symbols, sounds) that all alterations,

directing, focusing, and expansion of human consciousness
takes place. For Names guide and direct the mind, and it is
a well-known esoteric fact that the mind takes on the form of
the object it beholds and that the vital energies of man's
being run along the lines traced by the mind, energizing the
things or areas about which we think. A Word of Power is an
ideal, containing various psychological energies and materials
(intuitions, thoughts, feelings, and vital energies) which
are crystallized and concretized, projected by the will and
the imagination, and then introjected into the psyche so that,
temporarily, the operator can identify with it and serve as a
channel to manifest its attributes and energies in the world.

It is names, whether in religion, poetry, literature,
esoteric science, or even everyday speech, that bring about
the magic of inducing certain thoughts, feelings, and moods.
By the proper use of Names (words, images, sounds, symbols)
man can feel surprised, frightened, soothed, excited, joyful,
or depressed. By the proper use of names, man can learn and
teach, enlighten or confuse, direct others and be directed.
The power of names upon the human psyche and human behavior
is positively staggering. This fact has now been recognized
by theology, psychology, sociology, spiritual science, and
even common sense.

The Holy Scriptures, mythologies, legends, and great
masterpieces of world literature are all replete with countless
references and hints about the "miraculous" and "magical"
power of Holy Names, be they that of Krishna, Buddha, Mithras,
Osiris, Yahve, or Jesus. Both religious and mystical traditions have numerous and very explicit statements concerning the
importance of Divine Names. Thus, to cite just a few examples:

1. A Buddhist Psalm tells its devotees that: "There is no way
    into the Kingdom of Gladness save only by attaining unto
    the true faith through that Holy Name, the very Jewel of
    Wonder. . . the Holy Name of Buddha, of that Boundless
    Light that shineth into all the worlds of the Ten Regions,
    and the glory of His Kingdom destroys the darkness of
    ignorance in the Eternal Night, thus fulfilling all the
    longings of men."[4]

2. In the Christian Bible, Old and New Testament alike, we find
    a profusion of similar references, descriptions, and hints.
    Thus we have, for instance: "They that love Thy Name shall
    be joyful in Thee" (Psalms, 5. 12). "Thy Name is as oint-
    ment poured forth. . . draw me, we will run after Thee"
    (Zech. 10. 22). "I will glorify Thy Name for evermore"
    (Psalms 86. 12). "They have built Thee a sanctuary therein
    for Thy Name" (II. Chron. 20. 8).

3. Jesus Himself explicitly emphasized the power of Holy Names when He told His Disciples: "Whatsoever ye shall ask the Father in my Name, He will give it to you. Hitherto ye have asked nothing in My Name: ask and ye shall receive" (John 16. 23-24). "When two or three are gathered together in My Name, there I am in the midst of them" (Matt. 18. 20). And "In My Name shall they cast out devils; they shall speak with new tongues. . . . They shall lay hands on the sick, and they shall recover" (Mark 16. 17-18).

4. The Mystical tradition of the Eastern Church, known as the Hesychast tradition, is well-known to have anchored its search for spiritual enlightenment around the "Way of the Name," or the Jesus Prayer, as it is better known. This tradition has accorded explicit and primary importance to the practice of the Holy Name which is used as the primary means to expand consciousness. Here, the Holy Name is that of Jesus Christ, embedded in the short ejaculation: "O Lord Jesus Christ, Son of God, Savior, have mercy upon me." This formula has many versions, the shortest of which is the single word "Jesus." This mantram, accompanied by the Sign of the Cross, is repeated over and over again by the devotee with different techniques of breathing, visualization, and concentration until his state of consciousness noticeably alters.

5. An Eastern contemplative who used this method writes:

"The Name Itself is a means of purification and perfection, a touchstone, a filter through which our thoughts, words, and deeds have to pass to be freed of other impurities. None of them ought to be admitted by us until we pass them through the Name, and the Name excludes all sinful elements. Only that will be received which is compatible with the Name of Jesus. We shall fill our hearts to the brim with the Name and thought of Jesus, holding it carefully, like a precious vessel, and defending it against all alien tampering and admixture. This is severe asceticism. It requires a forgetfullness of self, a dying to self, as the Holy Name grows in our souls and gives us a foretaste of what spiritual power really is."[5]

6. And the same contemplative concludes:

"When we separately consider the aspects or implications of the Name of Jesus, our invocation of the Name is like a prism which splits up a beam of white light into several colours of the spectrum. When we call on the "total Name" we are using the Name as a lens which receives and concentrates the white light.

Through the means of a lens a ray of the sun can
ignite some combustible substance. The Holy Name,
acting as a lens, can gather and direct the light
until a fire is kindled within us."[6]

The Mystery Schools and the Occult and Magical Traditions,
likewise, have the same basic teaching concerning the use of
Words of Power, but they couch it in different words and use
different techniques. Thus the Tree of Life, which is the
master glyph and the practical "workshop of the Western Spiritual Tradition," as well as being the blue-print of man's
psychic and spiritual anatomy and the diagrammatic exposition
of the universe, is activated in each of its 10 Sephiroth,
on the Four Worlds, by Names of Power. To activate each of the
10 Centers and to travel the 32 Paths that connect them, the
Initiate vibrates the Names of Gods, Archangels, and Angels
attributed to them. It is upon these Names of Spiritual
Power that the Initiate draws upon to cooperate with the
Divine Purpose and to consciously speed up his human and spiritual evolution--to create, complete, and perfect both himself
and the world. By vibrating a given Name of Power in a given
Center in one of the 4 Worlds, the Initiate actually suffuses
his spiritual and psychic anatomy with the Light and Energies
corresponding to that Power, and raises his consciousness to that
particular Plane, attracting into his Aura the highest essence
and energies of that Plane and Power. This is the reason why
the Neophyte of the Mystery Schools is solemnly admonished:
"By Names and Images are all Powers awakened and reawakened"
and that "Names of Power link one spiritually to the Beings
who are invoked and who become aware of that invocation."

In the Christian Church we find a parallel to the foregoing both in the office of Prothesis of the Orthodox Liturgy
and in the Rosary of the Roman Catholic Church. In the first,
every Spiritual Hierarchy, from the Holy Trinity to Angels,
are invoked by Name, while in the second, various names of
Gods, Angels, and Saints are also invoked and ejaculated several times for the same purpose, but without explaining why
they are doing so. The Hesychast tradition, previously mentioned, also claims that the Name of Jesus vibrated in the
human heart, from which it radiates and propagates like a true
spiritual sun in every cell and department of our little kingdom, gives it the "power of deification."

Thus, it is no wonder that the sacred axiom of the
Brotherhood of the Rosy-Cross enscribed on the vault of the
Adepts is "Jesus is my All" which, when uttered with faith
(i.e. concentration, understanding, and love) brings the
living Presence of Jesus not only in our hearts but, from
there, to every Center and cell of our being. Like the legendary archetype of the Order, Christian Rosy-Cross, the
advanced student of the Mysteries must learn to say, to experience, and to realize: "Jesus is my all and His Name is
the Mystery of my Salvation." Apostolic Christianity, likewise,

vouches explicitly and through many of its Saints for the Power of the Holy Name of Jesus to "cast out devils," to "heal the sick," to "speak in new tongues," and to attain to the Living Presence, i.e. to genuine Spiritual Initiation.

Why do Words of Power act in such a way and why is the Name of Jesus so important for the student of the Western Spiritual Tradition? Words of Power act as psychic lenses to focus all of man's psychic energies upon one central object. In making a powerful effort of the will and in giving of himself, man will also receive, from his own Divine Spark and from the forces of the cosmos drawn into him by the principle of "like attracts like." By offering the best of himself, his human consciousness: knowledge, love, and vital energies focused and directed through a Name, man will receive, from his own Divine Spark and from the Higher Planes, a vaster knowledge, a deepened love, and vitalized energies. In short, he will become, through a transformation and expansion of consciousness and a changed way of life, a new being.

The key to the operative part of using Names of Power effectively is to become united with, and the channel for, the Power which the Name represents, to make "the Word become flesh," i.e. to enable the consciousness and life for which the Name stands to find a channel through one's human consciousness so as to manifest their attributes and carry out their will on the physical plane. The specific process by which this is accomplished is the following: the Name or Word is merely a vehicle, a cup or chalice, for the life and consciousness, i.e. for the Spirit, which must fill it. It is the Spirit alone which gives the Name life, meaning, and power, which expands and unfolds from Plane to Plane to the Divine Plane itself.

The construction of the chalice of the Name on the Inner Planes, the formation of its thought-form in the Astral Light, involves the use of man's power of concentration and visualization, of meditation and adoration, of invocation and evocation. But the ensoulment of that "chalice" or "mould" in the Astral Light is the result of an answer to man's desire and longing for it; it is the fulfillment of man's love call for the Light by the free gift of the Spirit which pours Its life into it.

Thus it is that the form of the Name, its chalice, image, and color, is the product of human will, effort, concentration, adoration and visualization; while its ensoulment or "coming to life" is the result of man's faith and love and of God's free gift and expression of Himself; it is the product of the complete operation of uniting one's psyche with the Power behind the Name and of making the Word become flesh, i.e. offering one's psyche and body as Its Temple.

This process, therefore, involves both maximum human effort
and a free manifestation of the Light which can in no way be
"coerced" or "brought down" into manifestation.

Its operative key was explicitly hinted at in the story
of the three Magi coming to worship the Christ-child and in
the greatest of all Commandments. The Magi, representing
the royal and distinctive characteristics of human nature--
knowledge, love, and will--must worship the Christ-child,
the manifestation of the Divine Spark, by offering Gold,
Myrrh, and Frankincense, i.e. the best of human knowledge,
human love, and human energies which are thus transformed,
exhalted, and spiritualized. The Comandment of commandments:
"Thou shalt love the Lord they God with all thy heart (love),
all thy soul (will), and all thy mind (knowledge)" points to
exactly the same process. A process, moreover, which was
also symbolically described by the Mystery Schools in the
Alchemical operation utilizing Mercury (knowledge), Sulphur
(love), and Salt (will) to produce the Azoth or Elixir Vitae,
the higher spiritual consciousness.

The entity, or thought-form, which man has thus con-
structed will then become, according to his Faith, the Door
or Channel, through which the Divine Light of God, and all
corresponding vibrations in the cosmos, will pour forth upon
man and suffuse him (when the Name used is that of Jesus
Christ) with the Divine Wisdom of the Father, the Divine Love
of the Son, and the Divine Creative Energies of the Holy Spirit
in a Cross pattern which will slowly spread to all the Centers,
cells, and departments of his being, until every nook and
corner of his little Kingdom has been filled with the Light,
Life, and Love of God. Then, the subjective element (man's
human consciousness) becomes united with the objective element
(the Spiritual Light), the Word with the Spirit, the conscious
with the superconscious, and man with God, as aspiration is
answered by inspiration and invocation by evocation.

A Word of Power (and the Holy Name of Jesus Christ in
particular) is thus a "seed," or a "stone," a "light-bulb"
in us that has to come alive in us once it has been "planted,"
until it expands so as to encompass all of our being, making
our human consciousness the Temple for Its Spirit and a Living
Rosy-Cross.

In order that this supreme operation may be effective
and properly realized, the candidate must first purify, develop, and integrate his etheric, astral, and mental bodies,
for man's highest mental vibrations become the point of ingress for Divine Wisdom, as his highest emotions become the
point of ingress for Divine Creative Energies.

Each Name can be seen as possessing three basic dimensions: the physical, the psychic, and the spiritual which are given life and power by the Father, the Son, and the Holy Spirit. On the physical level, the Name is most often handed down to us by sacred texts or by the sacred traditions. On the spiritual level, the Name is given Life and Power by the Spirit which begets it. But on the psychic level, it must be forged and fashioned in our human consciousness to act as a channel between the Spirit and Matter, the superconscious and the conscious, by the conscious use of all of our psychological faculties.

A last point to be made here is that a Name must not only be concretized in the Astral Light by concentration and visualization but also fed and amplified by meditation and adoration, if it is to become ensouled and given life by the Spirit in contemplation. This means that the student must meditate regularly on the Name he is building into a Name of Power for himself; that he must seek to "link" the Name to what he knows, to what he is, to what he is doing in his daily life, and to what he is striving to become. He must uncover and make explicit the many meanings, implications, and correspondences the Name has for him personally. He must set it at the center of his attention and then "free associate," i.e. let all intuitions, thoughts, and feelings pertaining to the Name flow through his stream of awareness. For only thus will the Name become a true Name of Power for him, expand its meaning and reveal its deeper mysteries as the student's consciousness expands and unfolds.

Seen in this light, the Science and Art of Divine Names also becomes a primary way of developing the student's power of concentration, meditation, and contemplation. At the physical level, the student must learn how to concentrate his whole being (all his heart, soul, and mind) on the chosen Name, making it the primary focus of his attention to the exclusion of all else. At the psychic level, he should meditate up on it, free associating around it and turning it into a "filing cabinet" for all incoming intuitions, thoughts, and feelings relating to it. All the meanings, associations, and implications which are revealed to the student should then be integrated with what he knows, what he is, what he does, and what he hopes to become. At the spiritual level, he should contemplate the Name, pouring his love and life into it and receiving greater love and life from its Spirit, becoming a channel for its conscious expression in the world. The Name used in this fashion then becomes a true "Door" for its Spirit, its Life, and its Consciousness, which become an objective Presence and Reality to the student and which can act as a lens or filter for all his thoughts, emotions, intuitions, sensations, moods, and decisions.

As the student grows and matures, becoming proficient
in the use of Names of Power, he will eventually discover
that, at their source, if traced all the way to their roots,
all Divine Names can be found in One Name and that the
Spirit behind them is, indeed, One, Ineffable, and Universal.
As the late renowned Occultist Dion Fortune stated so many
times: "In One God there is all the Gods and behind all
the Gods and Goddesses there is One God." Karl von Eckartshausen
put it even better:

> "As infinity in number loses itself in the unit which is
> their basis, and as the innumerable rays of a circle are
> united in a single center, so it is with the Mysteries;
> their hieroglyphs and infinitude of emblems have the
> object of exemplifying but one single truth. He who
> knows this has found the key to understand everything
> and all at once. There is but one God, but one Truth,
> and one way which leads to this grand Truth. There is
> but one means of finding it. He who has discovered this
> way possesses everything therein; all wisdom in one book
> alone, all strength in one force, every beauty in one
> single object, all riches in one treasure only, every
> happiness in one perfect felicity. And the sum of all
> these perfections is Jesus Christ."[7]

This brings us to our next question: the use of the
Divine Name of Jesus Christ and why it is so special. To
the student of the Mysteries in the Western Tradition there
are, to be sure, many Divine Names and many Names of Power that
are highly relevant and effective (e.g. the Names of the
Trinity, Father, Son, and Holy Spirit; the Name of the Theotokus
Mary; the Name of Celestial Hierarchs and of Saints, and the
whole range of the Qabalistic Names of Power. But, amongst
all these, there is One very special and potent Name of Power,
that of Jesus Christ. As the New Testament puts it: "God
hath highly exalted Him and given Him a Name which is above
every Name. . . that at the Name of Jesus every knee shall
bow" (Phil. II. 9-10). And: "Neither there is Salvation in
any other, for there is none other Name under heaven given
among men whereby we must be saved." (Acts IV. 12).

The translation of the word Jesus means <u>Savior</u> and
that of the name of Christ means "the Anointed One," the
"Messiah." That is exactly what the Supreme Name of Power
should mean to every student of the Mysteries: salvation through
the coming and at-onement with the "Anointed One," the Christ-
within.

If to the first axiom of the Brotherhood of the Rosy-
Cross: "He is my all and His Holy Name is the Mystery of
my Salvation" we add its second axiom: "Jesus Christ, Man
and God," we shall have a direct hint as to the esoteric

meaning and impact of the Holy Name. Jesus Christ is the
archetype and the prototype for every human being--what we,
too, at the end of our earthly evolution, must and will
become.

He is our supreme Ideal and Savior. Jesus here can be
seen as the symbol of the human side of our nature, as the
Temple or set of coordinated vehicles (physical, emotional,
mental, and spiritual) we must build for the Divine Spark
in us so that It can become conscious of Itself and manifest
Its attributes of Divine Love, Divine Wisdom, and Divine Creative Energies in Creation. Christ, on the other hand, can be
seen as the symbol of the divine side of our nature, as our
very own Divine Spark or "Only Begotten Son of God," as the
Bible has it.

Jesus is our Savior for many reasons, chiefly:

1. Because He represents the perfected, fully actualized,
    and completed man: what we have to strive for and will
    eventually become.

2. Because the only true Salvation for man lies in going
    boldly forward towards a greater actualization of our
    human faculties and realization of our spiritual po-
    tentialities. The most important questions for all human
    beings (Who am I? Where do I come from? Why am I here?
    Why are certain things happening to me? How should I
    live? What should I aim for?) can only be adequately
    answered in the future through the actualization of human
    powers and in the realization of spiritual consciousness.
    Man can neither go back to the past nor stand still in
    the present. He must go boldly forward to find a new,
    greater, fuller and more conscious harmony than the one
    he lost (in the Garden of Eden, when he was living "in
    nature"). And, if he is to go forward, he must know what
    he is to become, he must have a Supreme Ideal for his
    Self of tomorrow, and that Supreme Ideal is embodied in
    the person, life and teachings of Jesus. Finally, the
    salvation, not only of the individual, but also of the
    Angelic beings also resides with man's achievement of
    full manhood, with man's realizing his perfection, which
    is to become Jesus.

Christ, on the other hand, is our Divine Spark, which
is the "Anointed One" in our complex nature, an integral
"Spark" or "Nucleus" of the Universal Spirit. He is the "One"
Who is to come in all, the Bridegroom of the Soul, the Only
Begotten Son of God, and the reason why our complex nature,
lower and higher, has evolved and is evolving in its earthly
pilgrimage. He is the only One Who can truly "initiate us,"

The Library
INTERNATIONAL CHRISTIAN
GRADUATE UNIVERSITY

49

grant us true peace and happiness, open the gates of Heaven, i.e. the higher states of spiritual consciousness, and provide the ultimate answers to the riddle of our being and of all else. He, man's Divine Spark, however, has also been known as "Atma," as "Osiris," as "Adonai," as the "spiritual Self" and by countless other names.

In psychosynthesis, Jesus is the perfect model for what Roberto Assagioli called self-actualization, as Christ is the perfect model for what he termed Self-realization. The Holy Name of Jesus Christ, which has been consecrated and built into a tremendous Word of Power in the psychic atmosphere of the earth, can help us accomplish, according to both the Occult and the Magical Tradition of the Mystery Schools and the Mystical Tradition of the Church, the following things:

1. Help us to cast out devils, in ourselves, in a given locale, and in others.

2. Help us speak in new tongues.

3. Help us to heal the sick--ourselves and others.

4. Help us to receive whatever we ask in His Name with Faith.

5. Help us and others to achieve Salvation.

6. Help us find and penetrate into the Inner Church, the Brotherhood of the Rosy-Cross.

What do these things really mean. Very briefly, they can be interpreted as follows:

a. To cast out devils is to transform negative thoughts and feelings, and unbalanced forces, into positive and balanced ones; to change our state of consciousness; and to perform a true alchemical operation of raising the lower into the higher, and transmuting vices into virtues.

b. To speak in new tongues is to transform, to expand our state of consciousness so that we can know, understand, and do things which we could not do before.

c. To heal the sick is to apply the Panacea, the Divine Light, in a higher state of consciousness, to heal physical, emotional, and mental diseases and spiritual blindness.

d. To ask in His Name and to receive what we asked for is to know what we should do and strive for, in the light of higher states of consciousness, and to have the strength to actually do it.

e. To achieve Salvation is to attain true spiritual
    Initiation or Illumination.

f. To find and to penetrate into the Inner Church, the
    Brotherhood of the Rosy-Cross, is to raise one's level of
    consciousness and vibratory level so that one can com-
    municate in "thought" with true Masters and Adepts and
    enter, with one's Inner Bodies, into the true Temple
    of Wisdom in the Inner Planes.

    Why and how can this be so? The central reason why
the Holy Name of Jesus Christ can perform these "transformations of human consciousness" and "miracles" is that
this Holy Name, when vibrated with Faith, focuses our whole
attention upon the divine in us and in the world; it stimulates
into activity key psychospiritual Centers; it blazes open a
channel and a "sympathetic rapport" between our superconscious and our conscious; and that it raises the vibratory
activity of our human consciousness to that of the spiritual
realms.

    It accomplishes this through a synthesis of human effort
rising from below and of Divine Grace flowing down from above;
through a psychospiritual process involving all of man's highest
human faculties and his male-female polarities; and through
the peculiar law that "like attracts like," and that man can
only comprehend and draw that which is outside and above him
by what is in him. As an advanced student of the Mysteries
put it:

    "The beginning of the practice of the Holy Name is our
    intense faith in the Lord as our personal Healer and
    Savior. All that really separates us from receiving
    deliverance through the Holy Name in all our tribulations
    is but our lack of faith. It is at the point where Liv-
    ing Faith and the dawning of the true knowledge of God
    appear in the student's consciousness that the Holy Name
    will bring peace, victory, and deliverance when the
    latter is tempted, exhausted, nervous, irritable, angry,
    worried, confused, or "led astray." A heart filled with
    the Light and Presence of the Name will not tolerate any
    negative thoughts, images, feelings, and desires; and should
    these come, they will be instantly repelled or transmuted
    as light dispells and transforms darkness. The Aura of
    the student then acts as a steel "armour," the armour of
    Light of the Soul filled with the Divine Light of God."[8]

In the words of a real Alchemist and Qabalist I once knew:

    "When we say "Jesus is my all," the Light of the world
    illuminates our whole visible and invisible bodies; the
    Light generated by the Holy Name is actually He, Himself.

He heals our spiritual blindness, expels our impurities, purifies our spiritual leprosy and raises
the dead and sleeping powers within us into living
forces. He is now crucified in us. He dies and is
gloriously resurrected as Conqueror within us. After-
wards, His personality lives in us and instructs us
in the exalted Mysteries until he has made us complete and ready for perfect regeneration--when He
mounts to heaven to send us from thence the Spirit of
Truth. It is at this point, our attainment of the
lowest grade of the true Adeptship of the Spirit, that
the subline Rosicrucian axiom "Jesus is my all" becomes
a living fact for us. . . . It is the theurgic thought-
power of the words "is my all" which causes His Light
to spread all over the visible and invisible anatomy of
man, tracing a Cross of Light, and bringing real and
vast alchemical changes in us."[9]

Finally, the Name is also a passport, a key, or door to
the rich pastures of the Inner Church, the Communion of Saints,
and the Brotherhood of the Rosy-Cross. As He, Himself, stated:
"When two or three of you are gathered together in My Name,
there I shall be in the midst of you." A true Initiate,
whenever he pronounces the Holy Name, feels to be in communion with all the Holy Ones and the Celestial Hierarchies who
labor for the spiritual progress of mankind. Thus, he adopts
the "Way of the Name" as the best method of establishing
conscious contact with the Holy Ones, with all those he loves,
near or far, "dead" or alive.

In conclusion, I can say that the Holy Name is the
simplest and most efficacious method to obtain actual contact
with God, with the Divine Spark in ourselves. This contact
and union is, indeed, the ultimate and most coveted goal towards which all the most profound and arcane Mysteries of mankind converge as into a center. In the words of Karl von
Eckartshausen: "Do you wish, man and brother, to acquire
the highest happiness possible? Search for Truth, Wisdom,
and Love. But you will not find these except in unity, and
this is Jesus Christ, the Anointed of God."[10] It is also
written, "Without Me, ye can do nothing." (John 15.5).

A good clue to the deeper meaning of the foregoing symbolic statement can be found in the following metaphor:
without a source of light, no man can see anything. To see
on the physical plane, it is necessary to have physical light.
The same holds true for the spiritual planes which, ultimately,
control and brought the physical plane into being. There,
a source of spiritual Light is as necessary as physical light
is on the physical plane. This spiritual Light, Life, and
Energy by which all things were created, are sustained, and will

eventually be perfected, is Jesus Christ, the Light of the world and of our souls. Jesus Christ, therefore, can be looked upon as light or electricity which are universal and with us always and everywhere. But, like light or electricity, in order that they may be expressed and used in this world, a vehicle of expression, a "little temple," a "light-bulb" is absolutely necessary. The Name of Jesus Christ is just such a "light-bulb," a "lens," as the Eastern Monk called it, or a vehicle of expression for the reception and manifestation of the Cosmic Principle. Actually, however, it is our human consciousness which is the true "light-bulb" and "temple" for the Light, Life, and Love of Christ and His Name is more like a "switch" or a "tuner" that brings the power through. Such a Name must "become flesh" in us and expand in us until our whole personality and human consciousness are permeated by It and become the "light-bulb," the Temple, of the Divine Spark in the world. And only repeated and daily use, with faith and reverence, will make it such.

CHAPTER VI

THE SIGN OF THE CROSS: ITS NATURE AND USE

The central premise of the Spiritual Tradition and the most important axiom of the Mystery Schools is that God dwells in man and that the only way in which man can ever "find God," have a genuine "experience of the Divine Presence," and achieve "union with God" is to look for Him within the upper reaches of his own being and consciousness. This most important of all spiritual truths was being taught by Apostolic Christianity and explicityly stated by some of the Fathers of the Christian Church, as it was hinted at or taught, more or less explicitly, by all world religions.

Thus, St. Paul in I. Cor. 3.16 states: "Know ye not that ye are the Temple of God and that the Spirit of God dwells in you." St. Paul went as far as specifying that the Spirit of God resides in the spiritual body of man (the superconscious or the upper reaches of human consciousness) and must be sought there and not in the natural body of man. St. Augustine tells us "Lord, I have sought you in all the temples of the world and lo, I found You within myself." To this he later added: "If a man does not find the Lord within himself, he will surely not find Him in the world." Sendigovius, likewise, reminded us that "though Christ a thousand times in Bethlehem be born and not in my own soul, my soul will not be saved."

There are many specific and practical ways by which a sincere and devoted person can come in direct contact with the Lord (i.e. with his own Divine Spark or spiritual Self) and thus benefit from His Energies, Guidance, and Presence. All the world religions have implicitly or, sometimes, even explicitly shown their devotees how to bring about this contact, communion, and finally union. Likewise, all the genuine Mystery Schools have specific teachings and exercises designed to achieve the foregoing. At the core of both approaches, the religious and the occult, we find what we have termed the "Seven Fundamentals of the Holy Wisdom" which contain all the necessary theoretical teachings and practical exercises to lead man to a true spiritual Illumination, which is the result of entering into conscious contact with the Divine within.

The first of the "Seven Fundamentals" is a knowledge and practical use of Divine Names, or Names of Power, which we discussed in our previous chapter. The second is the Sign of the Cross which is a special application of the use of Divine Names on the Tree of Life, which we shall analyze in detail in the present chapter. Before beginning our analysis of the Sign of the Cross, of why it is so important in spiritual life and of how it operates, let us briefly review the major insights we discussed in our last chapter concerning the nature and use of Words of Power:

1. Names of Power are words, or psychic media, which convey and elicit the various units of human consciousness which we call intuitions, thoughts, feelings, and vital energies.

2. Words are true "bundles of energy," "streams of focused thought and emotion," and "individualized units of consciousness." They are the lens which direct and focus our whole attention upon an aspect of reality, upon a certain object, power, or being. They are the catalysts which convey and elicit certain energies and states of consciousness in our Sphere of Sensation or field of consciousness.

3. Names of Power are the psychospiritual means by which we invoke a certain Presence, induce a certain state of consciousness, and focus our awareness. They are the means through which we recreate in ourselves (in our imagination or in the Astral Light) an "image" or "facsimile" of that which is without or above us, and by which the powers and energies that are outside of us can contact us and enter into our Aura.

4. Words are so important to man in all his activities, whether sacred or profane, because they are the means by which he can deliberately awaken and focus his energies, feelings, thoughts, and intuitions by an effort of the will.

5. Names of Power, therefore, are the key regulators and transformers, or "switches" of man's human consciousness and of his inner life. It is through them that all awakening, focusing, alteration, and expansion of human consciousness take place.

6. Divine Names have both an outer and an inner part, a letter and a spirit that gives life to the letter. These parts can be represented by a chalice (the form or letter) and by Light and Life (the force or spirit) that fills that chalice, for the mind of man takes on the form of the object it beholds and his energies run along the lines traced by the mind and enliven the things about which we think.

7. Names of Power have both a male and female polarity. They are "points of entry," or channels, through which higher energies and levels of consciousness can reach us. They are also "projectors," or channels through which we can manifest our energies and consciousness. Hence, they have been likened to a "ladder of Jacob" on which "angels" are ascending and descending.

8. To make a Word of Power come "alive in us" and become a channel for spiritual Light and Life that will transform our consciousness and then our lives and our being, rather than merely remain another name, abstraction, or sound, three elements are needed:

   a. To know the Word of Power and some of its basic meanings and correspondences.

   b. To meditate regularly upon it so as to expand the set of meanings and associations it has for us, and to relate it to our being and life so as to discover the personal message, or correspondences, it contains for us on different levels of consciousness.

   c. To use it with deep Faith (i.e. knowledge and love backed by concentration) for, ultimately, it is Faith that will connect it with its spirit and which will, therefore, make it come alive in us and become a living channel for the Power which it represents.

9. All of the above, pertaining to the nature and use of Names of Power, is synthesized and expressed in the central formula of the Western Spiritual Tradition upon which we should meditate regularly and check with our own personal experience and results, as it contains the "esoteric and practical secret" of the use of Names of Power: "By Names and Images are all Powers awakened and reawakened."

   When it comes to the Cross and the many rituals and practical exercises connected with it, the first thing we should do is to suspend, momentarily, our judgment and our associations of ideas and feelings about it as being a specifically Christian symbol more specifically associated with the Eastern and Western Catholic Churches. The Cross is, of course, also a Christian and particularly a Catholic symbol (for the Catholic Traditions have openly claimed and used it, though in an unconscious manner and, most of the time, without the slightest realization of its deeper and more practical implications) but it is also far more than that. The Cross is a universal symbol and,therefore, a truly catholic one, which can be found, in one form or another, and with different interpretations, in all the world religions and in all the genuine Mystery Schools.

The earnest seeker will find the Cross at the very
beginning of his spiritual journey, on the very threshold
of the Path, just as the true Adept and Saint will "wear it
on his breast" as the unmistakable sign of his spiritual
attainment. The true disciple will use the Cross and live
with it daily, learning how to formulate it in his Aura, throughout the long journey of his spiritual quest for union with God.
As one writer puts it succinctly:

"The Cross is one of the most universal of symbols, as
well as one of the most ancient that is known to exist.
It is found on the monuments of Egypt, which have come
down to our time, with an antiquity of more than 4,000
years. The Cross is found on the ancient sculptures of
Babylon and Nineveh, and on the ruins of Persia and India.
It has been used as a symbol long previous to the Christian
Era in countries then totally unknown to each other and so
distant from each other as China from Peru. It has been
used as a sacred symbol by the ancient peoples of Mexico
and North America, by the Druids and the hardy Norseman,
by the wandering tribes in Central Asia, and the islanders
of the Southern Seas."11

The whole world over, in different times, places, cultures
and religions, we can see the Cross symbol appearing in different
forms, bearing different names, and with different meanings and
interpretations attached to it. Thus we find, for example, the
Egyptian Crux Ansata or Ankth and several variations of it. Then
we find the Hebrew, Greek, Phoenician, and Chaldean Tau Cross.
Then comes the Mexican and North American Cross which closely
resembles the Egyptian Crux Ansata. Then we have the Buddhist
and the Indian Flyfoot Cross, or Swastika, which can also be
found in pre-historic times in Norway, Ireland, Scotland, England
Cyprus, and Egypt. It can be found in the Jewish Qabalistic
Cross, in the Druid Cross, in the Shamrock of Ireland, and in the
various Christian Crosses ranging from the Greek equal-arm Cross
the Calvary Cross, the Bishop's Cross, to the Papal Cross.

In the Mystery Schools, the Cross symbol also played a
central role and can be found in many forms, with different
attributions and rituals attached to it. Thus, we have the 4
cardinal points represented by a Cross, the 4 elements represented by a Cross, and the 4 Archangels represented by a Cross.
Moreover, several practical spiritual exercises are also found
to be based on the symbol of the Cross.

Why should the Cross be so important to man and what key
functions does it perform to make it a universal symbol the
antiquity of which is lost in the dawn of human culture? Modern
social science is now finally beginning to recognize what the
Holy Wisdom has been teaching for ages. Namely, that the essence
of man is not his body or his possessions but, rather, the life

that flows and expresses through his body. This life orig-
inates in the Spirit of man, manifests itself through his
psyche, and culminates in its expression through human consciousness.

The essence of man's self, which flows out of his Spirit,
is now seen as being knowledge, love, and life which proceed
from Divine Wisdom, Divine Love, and Divine Life. The key
functions of man's psyche which, taken together, constitute what
we call human consciousness, are: thinking, feeling, willing,
intuition, imagination, biopsychic drives, and sensations. The
primary functions of the human psyche, or human consciousness,
are recognized by modern social science to be: thinking, feeling,
and willing, which they call the cognitive, affective, and the
conative processes. These processes are linked with and seen
to express, more particularly than the others, the three attributes of the Self--Knowledge, Love, and Creative Energy. It is
in terms of these that man's behavioral expression of speaking
and acting are explained and they constitute the central focus
of anthropology, sociology, and psychology. To simplify matters,
we can say that the essence of man's being is Spirit, Soul, and
Body, expressing at the ontological level as Knowledge, Love,
and Life, and at the existential level as thinking, feeling, and
willing which express in speech and action, and which manifest
at the conscious, unconscious, and superconscious levels.

Religion, philosophy, and science, the three major systems
of human knowledge and approaches to Reality have all expressed
and recognized, in their own way and words, the foregoing. Thus,
religion states clearly that God is a Trinity: Divine Wisdom,
Divine Love, and Divine Creative Energy or Life, and that man
should worship God in spirit and in truth (i.e. subjectively and
objectively) with all his heart (feeling), with all his soul
(willing), and with all his mind (thinking). Philosophy, through
the works and expressions of different philosophers, has defined
man's being, or essence, respectively, as thinking, loving, and
creating. Thus we have:

a. Descartes: "Cogito ergo sum," I think, therefore, I am; the
                 more I think, the more I am; I do not think,I am
                 not.

b. Pascal: "Amo ergo sum," I love, therefore, I am; the more
                 I love, the more I am; I love nothing, I am nothing.

c. W. James: "Acto ergo sum," I do, therefore, I am; the more
                 I do, the more I am; I do nothing, I am nothing.

Science, in its classification and labelling of man, has
come to exactly the same conclusion as philosophy, though expressed in different words. Thus, it has labelled man:

a. Homo Sapiens, man the knower, seeing knowledge as the dis-
                  tinctive feature of human nature.

b. <u>Homo Adorans</u>, man the worshipper or lover, seeing love as the feature of human nature.

c. <u>Homo Faber</u>, man the doer, the creator, seeing creativity and activity as the distinctive features of human nature.

    Finally, social science, too, has clearly indicated that it views the essence of man, the explanatory and causal attributes of human behavior, as being:

a. The <u>cognitive</u> processes, expressing knowledge and thinking.

b. The <u>affective</u> processes, expressing love and feeling.

c. The <u>conative</u> processes, expressing will, life, or creative energy.

It is these processes that social science sees today as holding the explanatory keys for interpreting the whole range of human behavior--all of what man says and does. Thus, summarizing the foregoing in simpler words, I would say that:

1. The essence of man is what he knows, what he loves, and what he does, which consciously express the attributes of his spiritual Self through his human self.

2. There is absolutely nothing that man can do, in any area of life, which does not require some knowledge (awareness), some love (desire), and some life (creative energy). Therefore, the more man knows, loves, and can express himself creatively, the more he is and can act in this world to do whatever he wishes to accomplish.

3. As knowledge, love, and life define both what man is and what man does, and man is here on earth to become a fuller, more conscious, and creative being than he was, prior to incarnating here, (to achieve self-actualization, Self-realization, and union with God), the central purpose of his pilgrimage on earth is to become capable of knowing more, loving more, and creating more: to deepen, expand, and heighten his consciousness so as to live a more "holy" life which will culminate in the creation of a new being.

    This is precisely where the Cross, in its deeper implications and its practical applications, comes in. Thus, in the present chapter, I shall look at and analyze briefly 5 of the major theoretical implications and practical applications of the Cross ritual, namely:

1. The Cross as a means to consciously bring more spiritual Light and Life to man's field of consciousness, to link man's human self to his spiritual Self.

2. The Cross as a means to achieve self-mastery and true peace.

3. The Cross as a means to express one's Self creatively in the world.

4. The Cross as a means to awaken and activate all the psycho-spiritual Centers on one's Tree of Life and, thereby, to eventually achieve true spiritual Illumination and Union with God.

5. The Cross as a means to consciously integrate reality within oneself; God with humanity and nature, and the inner world with the outer world.

1. <u>The Cross Ritual as a means of consciously bringing more spiritual Light and Life to man, to link man's human self with his spiritual Self</u>.

It is perhaps in the Egyptian religion that we can find the most direct and explicit "exoteric" statement concerning the Cross and its inner and practical meaning. The Egyptians called the Ankth the <u>Sign of Life</u>, the "door" to awakening and renewed spiritual life. The Christians linked it with Salvation (which, esoterically, means spiritual Initiation), <u>Resurrection</u>, and <u>Regeneration</u>. In point of fact, the central purpose of the Cross ritual is precisely to awaken man's spiritual consciousness and spiritual life from its present "sleep" or latency, by activating certain key Centers on the Tree of Life. It is the most simple, direct, safe, and effective means by which man can shift the "gears" of his consciousness, tap the reservoir of latent spiritual energy that exists within him, and establish a conscious "bridge" or rapport between his conscious and super-conscious. It is through the Ritual of the Cross, that the leap is made between the "state of nature" and the "state of grace," between normal and spiritual consciousness, and that the Initiate links with his "contact point," or "switch of power" in the inner worlds.

At the beginning of any practical spiritual operation, therefore, it is the Sign of the Cross that is used to re-establish and to reaffirm the <u>Cross of Light</u> within one's Sphere of Sensation by which the <u>Divine Light</u> and Fire are reached and drawn down to suffuse man's entire psychic economy. As such, the Cross does indeed, as we shall see later, contain the practical keys for the process of spiritual regeneration, spiritual resurrection, and genuine spiritual Illumination.

From time immemorial certain bodily "locations" and "organs" have been linked with certain psychological and psychic attributes and expressions, and this not by chance or arbitrarily! Thus, knowledge and thinking have always been associated with <u>the head</u>; love and feeling have been associated with <u>the heart</u> (in contra-distinction with passion, or the lower emotions, which are linked with the solar plexus); and creative energy and life have been associated with man's <u>hands</u> and <u>shoulders</u> which are the "roots" whence the hands issue from the body.

When we remember that man does not only have a natural or physical body but also psychic and spiritual bodies (i.e. the etheric, astral, mental, and spiritual bodies) and that these "bodies" have corresponding "organs" or "centers" of activity, called Flowers of Lotus in the East and Roses in the West, the foregoing will begin to make a lot more sense. Four of the most important psychospiritual Centers are located precisely around the above mentioned areas: <u>The Crown</u> (Primum Mobile) overshadowing the head, <u>Harmony</u> (the <u>Sun</u>) overshadowing the heart and Mercy (Jupiter)and Severity (Mars) overshadowing respectively the left and the right shoulders. It is through these Centers, and not their physical counterparts (head, heart, and shoulders) that knowledge, love, and life, thinking, feeling, and willing manifest themselves. A Fifth Center, the <u>Kingdom</u> (the Earth) is also touched and activated as the shaft of Light and Life, descending from the head into the heart, is then extended to the feet where this Center is located. Thus the spiritual Center (the head) is connected with the psychic Center (the heart) and with the physical Center (the feet); God, humanity, and nature are linked in the inner <u>Axis Mundi</u>, and we become a channel and transformer for the Energies and the Life of the Spirit to flow, through our being, to humanity and to nature. And this brings us to the traditional Sign of the Cross of the Christians.

Here, the devotee touches his forehead with his fingers saying "In the Name of the Father"; then he touches his heart with his fingers saying "And the Son"; and finally, he touches his right and left shoulders with his fingers saying "And of the Holy Spirit." What he is doing, in fact, is directing all of his attention and psychic energies, through the help of his physical or astral hand, to his Head Center, Heart Center, and Shoulder Centers, wherein he vibrates three Divine Names. The reason for doing so should now be obvious: it is to awaken and activate these Centers, to correlate and distribute their various energies, and to suffuse, via the activity of these Centers, his whole Sphere of Sensation with the Light and Fire he is "drawing from on high."

The "Father" here is the symbol of Divine Wisdom, the "Son" of Divine Love, and the "Holy Spirit" of Divine Creative Energy. By vibrating these Names of Power with all the Faith he is able to muster in their corresponding Centers, what the devotee is, in fact, saying is, from the spiritual standpoint: "let the Divine Wisdom of God manifest through my Head Center," "Let the Divine Love of God manifest through my Heart Center," and "let the Divine Creative Energy of God manifest through my Shoulder Centers." From the human standpoint, he is saying: "let my highest capacity for knowing now manifest through my head," "let my highest capacity for loving now manifest through my heart," and "let my highest vital energies now dynamize my will and my whole being."

To the degree that the devotee is ready for this and in accordance with his Faith (degree of concentration, knowledge for what he is doing, and love for what he is doing), an immediate transformation and expansion of his thinking activities, of his feelings, and of his vital energies will take place, as each Center is activated and correlated with the others. In this way, the Sign of the Cross will serve as a practical exercise to awaken, stimulate, and intensify man's three onto-logical principles and the three major faculties through which these express themselves. As there is positively nothing that man can do which does not involve some degree of knowledge (awareness), love (desire), and creative energy (will), whatever he will be doing, he will do more consciously, creatively, and efficiently after having used the Cross Ritual. In the words of an advanced spiritual scientist:

"When we say 'In the Name of the Father' and place our fingers on the forehead, we actually point with our fingers to an important organ in our spiritual body just below the space where God dwells in us 'on high.' The vibration set up in motion by our loving thought about our heavenly Father activates the Divine Essence of the 'Crown' which pours into our Heart Center as a veritable though unseen Glory (Light). This activation of the 'Crown' itself is described by St. Peter: 'Ye shall receive a Crown of Glory.' When we say: 'And the Son' and place our fingers on our heart, we again actually point with our fingers to a space in our spiritual body where the Divine Light, in the words of the Prophet Isaiah, poured upon us from 'on high' is activating another spiritual organ suffusing us with the Divine Love of the Son. When we say: 'And of the Holy Spirit,' touching our right and left breast respectively, we activate those spiritual sensoria within us which manifest as the creative and vitalizing power of the Holy Spirit in our lives. Finally, when we say 'Amen' and join our hands together, mentally affirming the presence of the Triune God within us, we actually close the spiritual currents within the periphery of our spiritual body in order to maintain this awakening to spiritual awareness as long as possible."[12]

The Sign of the Cross, therefore, is a practical exercise designed to:

a. Draw the Divine Light and Fire, or spiritual Energies, from the Crown Center "on high" and to bring it down into the Heart Center as a shaft of white Light. In this Center, they are transformed and distributed to all the other Centers and parts of our being. As such, the Sign of the Cross awakens and activates 4 key Centers on the Tree of Life, causing spiritual consciousness to dawn within the sphere of our consciousness.

b. Enable the devotee to "switch gears of consciousness" to
    bring spiritual consciousness to operate in his psyche by
    a breakthrough of the superconscious into the conscious.

c. Tap the infinite reservoir of Energy and Life which re-
    sides in the Divine Spark and to link it with man's con-
    sciousness.

d. To activate man's highest capacity for thinking, feeling,
    and willing, enabling Divine Wisdom, Divine Love, and
    Divine Creative Energies to flow through him.

These are some of the reasons why St. Paul could say
about the Sign of the Cross: "For the preaching of the Cross
is to them that perish foolishness; but unto us who are saved,
it is the power of God." The Sign of the Cross, however, is also
vastly more than the foregoing which merely points to one of
its most elementary and important applications.

2. The Sign of the Cross as a means to achieve self-mastery and
    true peace.

In our foregoing explanation and analysis, we showed
how the Sign of the Cross could bring true self-knowledge to
man by awakening spiritual consciousness and linking him with
his spiritual Self through the activation of key psychospiritual
Centers. Now we shall briefly discuss how it is also a most
simple, practical, and effective means to achieve self-mastery
and harmony with one's spiritual Self, or spiritual psychosynthesis.

Self-mastery can be achieved only when three basic pre-
requisites exist:

a. One has gained a minimum of self-knowledge and self-understandi

b. One's human self is connected, to some degree, with one's
    spiritual Self which then becomes the Center, or integrating
    principle, of one's being.

c. The various planes and energies, one's superconscious,
    conscious, and unconscious, are properly correlated and
    equilibrated so that the power of the Spirit can express
    itself through them.

The Sign of the Cross, by awakening spiritual consciousness
in one's psyche, accomplished condition (a). By linking the
spiritual Self with the human self via a breakthrough of the
superconscious into the conscious, which then opens a channel
between them, the Sign of the Cross accomplished condition (b).
Finally, by setting up an "axis mundi" and an energy distribution
pattern from the spiritual to the physical plane, linking intuition, thinking, feeling, and willing, as well as the subjective

dimension with the objective dimension, the Sign of the Cross
accomplished condition (c). In the words of an advanced spiritual scientist:

"History tells us that when Emperor Constantine was about
to wage a decisive battle with his enemies, there appeared
to him in a vision the Sign of the Cross with the message
'In Hoc Signo Vinces' which means by this sign you will
conquer. . . .If you want to conquer your inner enemies
and acquire spiritual rulership over your mortal nature,
which is the goal of all true spiritual development, the
same Sign of the Cross is this very moment above you. Its
message is ever the same 'by this Sign you will conquer.'
Yes, take up His Cross as more than a mere 'dead symbol.'
Make it a living force in your consciousness, and you will
soon experience a foretaste of what St. Paul calls 'the
power of God.'"[13]

3. The Cross as the model par excellence for all creative
   processes and the means by which man's Self can express
   Itself in the world.

One of the most important and fascinating powers that
man shares, to a small extent, with God is the power to create,
to bring into being new things. To create anything, man needs
three basic ingredients that succeed each other, in the creative process, through three consecutive steps. These are:

a. Knowledge of what man wants. The formulation of an idea
   or picture of the new reality to be brought about.

b. Love or a strong desire for that particular idea or picture
   to be realized.

c. The will or energy necessary to realize it and to translate
   the idea into an objective reality.

Thus, the creative process involves an idea vitalized by
love which then sets in motion the energies of the will which
will bring about its realization. This process is directly
related to the Ritual of the Cross, following its exact sequence.
Thus the knowledge, the ideas and pictures, are "hatched" in
the Head Center, the love or desire flows out of the Heart
Center while the energies necessary for its realization are
drawn from the Shoulder Centers, and their interrelation is
brought about by tracing the Sign of the Cross.

To use the Ritual of the Cross as a model for any creative
endeavor, the following steps should be followed:

a. The devotee should begin by tracing the Sign of the Cross
   upon himself to awaken his key faculties and their related
   Centers by forming a Cross of Light within his Aura.

b. Then the devotee should turn to the "Father" with all
his Faith by concentrating on the head region to obtain,
from Divine Wisdom, all the necessary inspiration he needs
to formulate and concretize a given ideal or end. He
should ask of Divine Wisdom, by continuing his meditation
on the head Center, all the necessary inspiration and knowledge to concretize this idea, or image, which he should
visualize vividly.

c. Once the ideal and its idea, or image, are clearly formulate
and visualized, the devotee should turn to the "Son" with
all his Faith by concentrating on the heart region, to
obtain from Divine Love all the necessary love and desire
to fertilize that ideal and its representation.

d. Finally, when the devotee feels at one with his ideal and
image, once they have been indrawn into him, as it were,
from being first objectified outside of him, he should then
turn to the "Holy Spirit" with all his Faith, by concentrating on the shoulder region, to obtain from Divine Creative Energies all the will power or creative life force he
needs to realize and objectify this ideal in the world
through his actions.

e. Should at any time the ideal, or its image, weaken, become
ambiguous, vague, or confused during the process necessary t
realize this ideal empirically, the devotee should turn to
Divine Wisdom (in the Head Center) to receive fresh inspiration, knowledge, and the power to concretize his visualizat
Should his love or desire for this ideal weaken, become am-
bivalent, or torn between other goals and ends, he should
turn again to Divine Love (in his Heart Center) to receive
an intensification and deepening of his love and desire for
it. Finally, should his will or energies become "sapped"
or depleted, or be insufficient for the task at hand, he
should then turn again to Divine Creative Energy (in the
Shoulder Centers) to receive fresh life forces and a vital-
ization and strengthening of his will power, and resolve to
accomplish that end.

4. The Cross as a means to awaken and activate all the psychospiritual Centers on the Tree of Life and, thereby, to
eventually achieve true spiritual Illumination with God.

Another very important and basic practical exercise based
on the Ritual of the Cross is the Qabalistic Cross. This is an
exercise drawn from the mystical tradition of Israel (hence eith
Hebrew or English words may be used) which has been adopted and
largely used by all legitimate Mystery Schools in the West.

For this use of the Ritual of the Cross, the devotee shoul
begin by breathing deeply a few times, by relaxing physically
and mentally, and by preparing himself inwardly. Then he should

turn to the spiritual East and point with his fingers to his
Head Center saying "A TEH"(For Thine). Visualizing a shaft
of brilliant white light flowing out of his Head Center, he
should direct it, with his attention and fingers, to his Feet
Center saying "MALKUTH" (is the Kingdom). He should feel
the Light and Life of the Crown flowing down to his feet,
awakening his Feet Center with an unmistakable sensation. In
so doing, an "axis mundi," a shaft of Light, or psychic channel,
will be established from head to foot, connecting the superconscious with the conscious and the unconscious (Heaven, Earth,
and Hell), the spiritual Self with the human self and the biopsychic nature of the devotee. In so doing, all the Centers on
the Middle Pillar will be affected and activated to a certain
degree. The spiritual Self will then consciously bring Its
vitalizing and synthesizing energies throughout the devotee's
entire being, thus establishing a life current between the two
terminal Centers on the Tree of Life, the spiritual and the
physical, affirming and establishing the rulership of the Divine
Spark in the devotee's "little Kingdom."

     After a living response and awakening has taken place and
has been experienced by the devotee, after the shaft of Light
connecting the head and the feet has been firmly established
and felt by the devotee, the latter should point his fingers to
his right shoulder saying "VE GEBURAH" (and the power) to awaken
that Center, and trace a horizontal shaft of pink-purple light
to his left shoulder where he should vibrate the Name "VE GEDULAH"
(and the Glory). In so doing, he will not only bring the Divine
Light, Fire, and Life, the spiritual Energies, down into his
human psyche and consciousness, affirming the rulership of the
divine principle in him, but he will now also be able to use
these energies and inspirations constructively and creatively
in his being and in his life, in a balanced and equilibrated way.
Here a connection and synthesis will be effected between the male
and female principles in him, between Severity and Mercy, just as
a connection and synthesis is effected between the Spiritual and
the Physical principles, the Crown and the Kingdom, in him,
through the vertical shaft of Light. Moreover, the integration
and synthesis between Worship (climbing on the "Sacred Mountain"
on the vertical axis) and Service (using the Light and Fire
received on the "Sacred Mountain" to help and enrich the lives
and beings of others) will also be affirmed and strengthened.
Finally, the rhythm between Prayer (vertical axis) and Living
the Life (horizontal axis) will also be brought to consciousness
and will be emphasized.

     Man's "little Kingdom," the billions of cells, entities,
energies, and principles that dwell, consciously, unconsciously,
and superconsciously in him, do belong to the spiritual Self
who will rule them and synthesize them eventually. The power
and the life of man should also be consecrated to the God within
and to the completion of the Great Work--which is what this Ritual
in fact affirms and temporarily realizes in the devotee.

This Ritual should then be completed by bringing both
hands to touch each other in the center of the devotee's chest,
wherein he will vibrate the words "LE OLAM AMEN" (may it be
so forever) which closes the circuit of Light and Life within
his Sphere of Sensation and which preserves and strengthens
the Cross of Light which is glowing in him.

When this exercise is carried out with full consciousness
and attention, and with living Faith, it will temporarily induce a brief glimpse of genuine spiritual Illumination and
at-onement between the spiritual Self and the human self of the
devotee, thus giving him a foretaste of what will eventually
happen to him on a permanent basis and helping him to get a
little closer to that great goal.

5. The Cross as a means to integrate reality within oneself;
    God with Humanity and Nature, and the inner world with the
    outer world.

The Sign of the Cross is also the means by which the devote
can establish a true axis mundi within himself (a shaft of Light
or Energy connecting the superconscious, the conscious, and the
unconscious) through which all levels of Reality and all Powers
can be contacted and linked with each other: the Spirit of God
through the awakened Head Center, Humanity through the Heart
Center, and Nature or the body through the Feet Center. In this
ritual, therefore, God, the Father, Nature, the Mother, and
Humanity, the Son, are invoked and synthesized in the consciousness of the devotee, and the inner work, or introversion, is
correlated with the outer work, or extroversion. The higher
Energies of the Spirit (the Divine Light, Fire, and Life) are
brought from the head to the heart where they are radiated to
Humanity, and from the heart to the feet where they are radiate
to Nature, thus linking the subjective world of the devotee (his
Sphere of Sensation of field of consciousness) with the objectiv
world of Humanity and Nature.

There are many other special applications and variants
of the Ritual of the Cross, just as there are many more correspondences, meanings, and treasures connected with it on differe
Planes of Being and states of consciousness. But these will hav
to be discovered by the devotee himself, through his own personal experience and exploration of them. Enough has been said
in this chapter to launch a sincere seeker and to guide him on
his way to this personal discovery.

It has rightly been said that "the mystery of life is not
a problem to be solved but a Reality to be experienced." Likewise, the secrets and treasures of the Cross Ritual are not ab-
stractions to be discussed or written about, but Powers and
Realities to be directly and personally experienced.

CHAPTER VII

THE LORD'S PRAYER: ITS NATURE AND USE

In this chapter, I shall look, briefly, at the nature, function, purpose, and practical use of the Lord's Prayer so as to make it come "alive" within the consciousness and life of the devotee. Please bear in mind that my purpose is not to tell you what it is, for that you will have to discover yourself from personal experience. My aim is to increase your reverence for an appreciation of it, and to motivate you to use it frequently with some understanding of its function, purpose and practical applications, so that it may reveal its mysteries and treasures to you as it has to me.

I. The nature of the Lord's Prayer (what it is): the Lord's Prayer is a related set of symbols, or formulae, containing both knowledge about man's psychospiritual anatomy and physiology, and an integrated set of practical exercises designed to awaken man's psychospiritual Centers, train key human and spiritual faculties, "nourish" his entire psychospiritual nature, and achieve spiritual Illumination or Union with the Divine Spark or spiritual Self.

II. The functions of the Lord's Prayer (how it operates): the Lord's Prayer must be activated in man's field of consciousness. But from there it can also function in and affect the subconscious and the superconscious mind through its language of images and archetypes. The key faculty that makes the Lord's Prayer effective and "living" is Faith, as it is for any other ritual.

III. The purpose of the Lord's Prayer (what it can do): the Lord's Prayer has many purposes operating on different levels. Here are some of the major ones:

1. Psychologically: it can be used to awaken man at the psychological level, to focus his attention and the various functions of his psyche upon whatever he is about to undertake.

2. Socially: it can be used to unite the aspirations, thoughts, feelings, and energies of a group of people, and thus to achieve social integration and interpersonal psychosynthesis.

68

3. <u>Spiritually</u>: it can accomplish many things, chief of which are:

    a. Provide man with a living source of knowledge.

    b. Enable man to train and exercise various psychological and spiritual faculties and thus to develop them.

    c. Progressively awaken, activate, and integrate all the psychospiritual Centers.

    d. Establish a genuine breakthrough of the superconscious into the conscious and open up a channel between the human and the spiritual Self through which inspirations and energies can flow.

    e. Feed and correlate all of man's "bodies" and their key faculties, spiritual, mental, emotional, and vital.

    f. Progressively enable man to link his will with the Will of the Divine Spark within him so that the latter may manifest Itself in the world and express therein the attributes of the spiritual Self--Divine Wisdom, Love, and Life.

    g. Provide a safe and effective way of coming in contact with the Inner Worlds, the Celestial Hierarchies, and the Brotherhood of the Rosy-Cross.

    h. Eventually achieve spiritual Illumination and union with the spiritual Self, or spiritual psychosynthesis, which is the goal of human evolution and the highest aim of all genuine spiritual training. As this union of man's conscious self, or ego, with the spiritual Self, or Divine Spark, is accomplished in slow degrees by consciously and actively pursuing it, his whole being will come to life and he will lead an increasingly more conscious, creative, useful, and happy life.

IV. <u>How to use the Lord's Prayer</u>: the Lord's Prayer can be used by oneself or in a group. To use it one should relax, breathe deeply, and use the Ritual of the Cross, and then begin. Basically, the Lord's Prayer can be used for 4 concrete and specific objectives:

    1. <u>To develop key human faculties</u>: concentration, visualization adoration, coordination and balance, and psychosocial integration.

    2. <u>To practice meditation and contemplation</u> and, thereby, expand one's knowledge of its key meanings, correspondences, and applications, and of one's being, psychospiritual anatomy and physiology.

3. <u>Theurgically</u> as a key Light, Fire, and Life bringing and consciousness and energy transforming ritual to link aspiration and inspiration, invocation and evocation.

4. <u>To practice, construct, and project a major set of thought-forms</u> which can become a vital and magnetic center in one's being and life, and in that of others.

Thus one can:

a. Concentrate and meditate on each key symbol of the Lord's Prayer and then contemplate and experience its "awakening and response" in one's consciousness.

b. Concentrate and meditate on each petition of the Lord's Prayer and then contemplate and experience its impact on each Center of the Tree of Life, and on each "body" and "level of consciousness."

c. Concentrate and meditate on the whole prayer and then contemplate and experience its impact upon one's whole being, consciousness, and daily life.

V. <u>Key work in meditating on the Lord's Prayer</u> and deciphering its key meanings, correspondences, and applications.

<u>Text of the prayer</u>:

Our Father who art in heaven. Hallowed by Thy Name. Thy Kingdom come. Thy will be done, on earth as it is in heaven. Give us this day our daily bread, and forgive us our trespasses as we forgive those who trespass against us. And lead us not into temptation but deliver us from evil (the Evil One). Amen.

1. <u>Our Father who art in Heaven</u>.

    a. Key symbols: Our, Father, Heaven.

       <u>Father</u>: The "Father" is the creative and life sustaining principle, the spiritual principle whence we came, which sustains our lives while here, and to which we shall eventually return in full consciousness. The "Father" is the real, immortal, spiritual, but as yet unknown Self; it is the Divine Spark, the Christ-within, Osiris, Atman, the Lord, or whatever the God-in-man is called.

       <u>Heaven</u>: It is a higher and qualitatively different state of consciousness than the one we are normally functioning in, it is spiritual consciousness or the superconscious.

Our: We all come from the same spiritual Source, are made of the same spiritual Essence, and will eventually achieve the same union with the spiritual Self. This symbol implies, therefore, the Fatherhood of God and the Brotherhood of man, and affirms that the spiritual Self is One and at-one with the same cosmic principle.

b. As a whole, this petition focuses our consciousness (aspirations, thoughts, feelings, and energies) upon our Divine Spark, opening up a channel through which the Divine Light and the spiritual Energies can flow into our whole Aura, and it establishes a breakthrough of the superconscious into the conscious. In so doing, we "light the Lamp on high" or "put on our Crown," i.e. we activate Kether. This is the key "switch" by which the Initiate turns on his "contacts" and the disciple contacts the latent spiritual energy and will that lies dormant within himself.

c. This petition thus leads us to the realization of God's Presence within our being and in the world; it blazes open a psychic channel or "ladder of Jacob" through which we can rise to Him and enable His Wisdom, Love, and Life to express themselves in our being, in our lives, and in the world.

2. Hallowed be Thy Name.

a. Key symbols: Hallowed be, Thy Name

Hallowed be: implies to become aware of, to enter into a proper relationship with, and to give and take what is appropriate.

Thy Name: The Presence, Consciousness, and Energies of the Divine Spark. A name is a representation of and a path to the reality that it represents; in this case, the spiritual Self.

b. This petition reaffirms and deepens the breakthrough of the superconscious into the conscious established by the first petition, and it draws down the Divine Light and Fire by one's hunger for it and devotion to it. While with the help of the first petition we climbed onto the "Sacred Mountain" of consciousness to the place where the Divine Light and Presence dwell, with the present one we draw down and "bring back" that Light and Presence into the field of consciousness, and we suffuse our whole being with It (i.e. our spiritual, mental, emotional, and vital "bodies").

c. This petition formulates a Cross of Light in our Aura distributing and spreading the Light and Energies, and thus the Consciousness, of the Divine Spark in all the dimensions, nooks, and cranies, of our being. Likewise, it also helps every "body," principle, and subpersonality in our being to become aware of an enter into a proper relationship with the down-pouring Light of the spiritual Self. It awakens Chockmah and Binah, thus slowly bringing His Consciousness and Presence in our field of consciousness and life, purifying, sanctifying, and perfecting both the human temple and the world.

3. Thy Kingdom come.

   a. Key symbols: Thy, Kingdom, come.

   Kingdom: This symbol literally means a king ruling over a body of men occupying a certain territory which is governed by certain laws. In this petition, the "Kingdom" is our personality with its functions, faculties, energies, and many entities. Thus far, the King (the Divine Spark) is not ruling yet, or is ruling only in an indirect and partial way. The reason that the Divine Spark is not ruling our personality is that the channel between the superconscious and the conscious is not fully developed and operative, the connection between the human and the spiritual Self is tenuous, the personality itself is not completed or well coordinated, and many other principles are still ruling our being and lives.

   Thy: Refers to the Divine Spark, the spiritual Self.

   Come: Let that come into being, be realized in our life. That is, let the spiritual Self become the King, Lord, or synthesizing principle of our personality and life.

   b. This petition again draws down the Divine Light and Energies of the spiritual Self in a Cross-like fashion, activating Chesed and bringing the awarenss of the Presence and Rulership of the Divine Spark in all the levels of consciousness and aspects of our being.

   c. This petition also helps us to realize and to experience that the "Kingdom of God" is a state of consciousness which must be realized within oneself and which will then radiate into, affect, and transform our personal, professional, social, and spiritual life. It makes us aware that this is the greatest goal and treasure we can and must achieve here on earth, and it brings with this awareness the strength to realize it, little by little.

4. <u>Thy will be done, on earth as it is in heaven</u>.

    a. Key symbols: Thy Will, be done, Earth, Heaven.

        <u>Thy Will</u>: The will or focused energies of the Divine Spark.

        <u>Be done</u>: Accomplished, translated from potentiality into actuality, brought from the level of an idea to that of an experience, realized in our being.

        <u>Earth</u>: Our field of consciousness, our conscious mind our personality and body.

        <u>Heaven</u>: The superconscious, the higher, superliminal levels of consciousness, or spiritual consciousness, wherein one truly knows oneself, God, one's fellow-men, and one's purpose on earth.

    b. This petition, through another outpouring of spiritual Light and Energies, continues and objectifies the process begun by the former petition. If God's Kingdom is to be realized in our being, in our lives, and, finally, in the world, His Will must be accomplished as a prerequisite for that. God's Will, the Will of the Divine Spark, is always being accomplished in the superconscious, in the spiritual nature of man, but not in his personality, in his conscious mind. What takes place at the superconscious and spiritual levels must now be extended and projected, as well as realized, at the conscious and personality level, through a desire for and cooperation of the latter. Once God's Presence has become conscious in us, His creative Energies or Will can gradually become operative in our personality and life. The thought-form contained in this petition is designed to have us focus on this operation so as to realize it consciously.

    c. In a third down-pouring of Light and Life through the great Cross of the Tree, Geburah is now activated and energized; intuition, the flow of spiritual Consciousness and Energies, now fuse with our aspirations, thought and feelings spiritualizing them and thus transforming our words and actions. "Be done" here refers to the transmission and transformation of the Divine Light through the various "bodies" (from the spiritual to the mental, from the mental to the emotional, and from the emotional to the vital and physical) to accomplish the purpose of the spiritual Self. It is also the theurgic formula to actually bring the Light and Energies of the Divine Spark from Heaven to Earth, from Spirit to Matter, from Kether to Malkuth.

73

5. <u>Give us this day our daily bread</u>.

   a. Key symbols: Give us, this day, daily bread.

      <u>Give us</u>: Suffuse our being (Aura and Tree of Life) and let us become aware of.

      <u>This Day</u>: Now, wherever we happen to be, the present cycle in our evolution.

      <u>Daily Bread</u>: On the horizontal axis, the daily bread of our soul is <u>experience</u>, on the vertical axis, it is the <u>Divine Light</u>.

   b. Every day, in every cycle, at every moment of our lives, the Divine Spark gives us the "daily bread" of our soul, human experience, but we are not aware of this, we do not understand what is happening to us or why we are living through our present situation and, therefore, cannot appreciate it and assimilate it fully. On the vertical axis, this petition theurgically brings down the Divine Light into the Tree of Life and our field of consciousness so as to make us understand our daily experience, be able to assimilate it more fully, and learn the lessons that it brings to us, and thus be grateful to God for it--to receive it and accept it as a gift of God and an opportunity for our human and spiritual growth.

   c. This petition, through a fourth down-pouring of Light and Energy via the Cross of the Tree, activates Tiphareth and makes us more "alive" and aware of the great gift that life and its countless daily experiences truly are, of the myriad opportunities that come our way to learn, to grow, to serve others and thus to live more consciously, creatively, and joyfully.

   d. The thought-form contained in this petition opens up our consciousness and receptivity to the Divine Light coming from "on high" and to the world "around us" and thus helps us become more alive, responsive, and coordinated as a Temple of Life and Consciousness.

6. <u>Forgive us our trespasses as we forgive those who trespass against us</u>.

   a. Key symbols: Forgive us, trespasses, we forgive.

      <u>Forgive us</u>: The spiritual Self always forgives us our trespasses and transforms our errors and mistakes into experiences and lessons that, ultimately, will benefit us and enable us to mature, to improve, and to transform our imperfections. But, most of the time, we are unaware of this.

<u>We forgive</u>:   It is we who, many times, do not forgive
others and, therefore, ourselves, and live
with a heavy burden of anger, resentment,
and lowered vibrations.

<u>Trespasses</u>:   These imply the violation of physical,
psychological, social, and spiritual laws
in deeds, words, emotions, thoughts, or
aspirations.

b. This petition makes us aware of a most important universal law: that of action and reaction, or cause and
effect, Karma, which takes place on three levels:

   1.   Between the superconscious and the conscious mind,
the spiritual and the human self, as well as the
conscious and the unconscious mind.

   2.   Between our state of consciousness and our deeds,
between our thoughts and our actions.

   3.   Between ourselves and the world, which includes
other human beings, animals, and nature; between the
subjective and the objective dimensions of life.

c. This petition shows us that what we do unto others,
ultimately, we do unto ourselves, that any objective
action in the world is immediately followed by a reaction in our consciousness and personality.   It shows
us, therefore, that as we forgive others, we forgive
ourselves, and thus become aware that the Divine Spark,
too, has forgiven us.   In this life, we constantly
violate a number of physical, psychological, social, and
spiritual laws, some of which we are aware of and others
of which we are not aware, some that we could have obeyed,
and others which, at our point in evolution and with our
present level of consciousness, we could not have obeyed
as yet.   Thus, we are much in need of forgiving and being
forgiven.   This is the reason why Jesus admonished His
Disciples "forgive them their trespasses not 7 times but
70 times 7 times.

d. True forgiveness implies a great deal more than simply
saying "I forgive you, let us begin anew in a different
frame of mind."   It implies mental understanding, emotional release, behavioral acceptance, and spiritual
"connection" and perspective.   It involves "unclogging"
psychospiritual Centers, transmuting many thoughts, emotions, and energies, and actually changing our state of
mind.   It involves dissolving unbalanced forces, negative
thoughts and emotions in our Aura and then in that of

others who come to us with their problems and re-
sentments. It means actually transforming vices into
virtues and thus performing a genuine alchemical operation in ourselves and then in others.

e. This is made possible by a fifth down-pouring of spiritual Light and Energies which diffuse through the Cross
on the Tree and focus this time upon Netzach, awakening
and activating it. In its wake, this further out-pouring
of spiritual Light and Energies, brings a playfulness,
a lightness, an acceptance and tolerance which are not
weakness or unconcern, but a larger perspective on things,
which is unmistakable by the joyfulness and exhuberance
they make possible in he who has truly forgiven himself
and others.

7. Lead us not into temptation but deliver us from evil (the
Evil One)

a. Key symbols: Lead us not, temptation, deliver us, evil
(one).

Lead us not: Make us aware of, recognize, and be grateful
for. . . temptations

Temptation: The inevitable tests and trials of life we
must all face.

Deliver us: Give us the awareness, understanding, and
strength to overcome temptations when they
come to us and learn the lessons which they
contain.

Evil (One): This is our lower self, unbalanced forces,
negative thoughts, emotions, and energies
in our being which must be conquered and
eventually transformed into a pure vehicle
for the Higher Self.

b. Of all the petitions of the Lord's Prayer, this is the
one that is most apt to be misunderstood, probably because of a poor translation of the original words and
meanings. The spiritual Self never leads us into temptation; it is our lower self, our conscious self, which
does this. Temptations, moreover, abound in life and
are necessary for our human and spiritual growth! The
key here is to be aware that a temptation is such, i.e.
a test sent for our benefit, and to have the wisdom and
the strength to resist it and thus pass this test suc-
cessfully. Temptations are myriad and of many different
types. Some are physical while others are emotional,
mental, and even spiritual; some are within our power
to resist, others are not and can only be overcome with
spiritual assistance.

c. This petition, therefore, is an invocation of the
    spiritual Light to help us recognize temptations for
    what they are, to have the strength to withstand their
    onslought, and the wisdom to be grateful for them.
    Basically, there are two types of temptations: those
    created by our lower self (the great majority) and those
    sent to us by God as a test and our next lesson on the
    Path (which are still fairly rare for the majority of
    people).

d. This petition, through a sixth down pouring of the spir-
    itual Light and Energies via the Cross on the Tree of
    Life, activates Hod and Yesod respectively and gives us
    the awareness, perspective, and strength to overcome the
    dark side of our nature, the "shadow" or personal "Devil"
    which is made up of the accretion of all our vices, wrong
    deeds, and negative thoughts, emotions, and energies ac-
    cumulated and crystallized over a long period of time.

8. <u>For Thine is the Kingdom, and the Power, and the Glory, of th</u>
    <u>Father and of the Son, and of the Holy Spirit</u>.

    Though some churches do not use this ascription as part of
    the Lord's Prayer, or omit it altogether; from the esoteric
    view-point, it is an integral part of it; it is its very
    conclusion and culmination.

    a. Key symbols: For Thine, Kingdom, Power, Glory, Father,
                      Son, Holy Spirit.

        <u>For Thine</u>: The Kingdom, ultimately, is of and for the
                      Divine Spark.

        <u>Kingdom</u>:   Man's conscious mind, personality, Malkuth.

        <u>Power</u>:   Refers here to certain spiritual Energies
                      activated in Geburah and expressing the Will
                      and Justice of God.

        <u>Glory</u>:   Refers here to other spiritual Energies ac-
                      tivated in Chesed or Gedulah, expressing the
                      Love and Mercy of God.

        <u>Father, Son, and Holy Spirit</u>: These are the Trinity, One
                      in essence and threefold in manifestation, i.
                      the Divine Light expressing as Divine Wisdom,
                      Love, and Creative Energy or Will.

    b. This petition is both the culmination and the completion
        of the Lord's Prayer, and the Christian version of the
        Qabalistic Cross. As the Lord's Prayer began with the
        Cross Ritual so it ends with it.

c. This petition now "fixes" the Cross of Light, which
    has been awakened and formed through successive down-
    pourings of Light and which has activated all the
    psychospiritual Centers, upon the Aura of the devotee
    who now "wears it on his breast". . . when he has be-
    come a true Initiate.

d. This petition also states in symbols and builds up a
    final thought-form, asserting (and thus bringing about
    in the mental worlds) that the Kingdom and its Powers
    (man's conscious mind, personality, life, and the
    functions of his psyche) are of and for the spiritual Self
    to become conscious of Itself and to manifest Its at-
    tributes of Divine Wisdom, Divine Love, and Divine
    Creative Energies in man and in the world.

e. Having gone down the entire Tree of Life through the
    "Path of the Flaming Sword," this seventh and final
    down-pouring of spiritual Light and Energy now focuses
    upon Malkuth, awakening it, activating it, and dedi-
    cating it to the work of the Divine Spark which it must
    reflect and perform in this world. It also opens up
    the "Path of the Sword," or the Path of return, through
    which our daily experiences and lessons can be assim-
    ilated by our soul and our spiritual Self.

Conclusion: We have seen how the Lord's Prayer contains a true
philosophy of Man, God, and Nature, and a practical art, or set
of exercises, to awaken, activate, and nourish all of man's
"bodies," all of the psychospiritual Centers on the Tree of Life,
and all of the functions of the psyche. As such, it contains a
whole program of spiritual science in a nutshell, having its
functional equivalents in other religions and traditions, and
containing all the knowledge and exercises necessary for man to
reach true spiritual Initiation, the union of his human with
his spiritual Self, and genuine Illumination.

The Initiates of Ancient Greece claimed, in their Mystery
tradition, that Divinity is entombed in nature, that It sleeps
spell-bound in man, and that man's greatest and highest labor
here is to break that spell and to open that tomb so that the
Divine can reawaken and manifest consciously Its attributes in
Creation. The Lord's Prayer is, therefore, the practical key
to accomplish this Herculean labor. But, as the Lord's Prayer
is made living and effective by man's Faith, and as it reflects
his level of evolution and consciousness in how it is used and
interpreted, man will probably have to use it thousands of times
before its true import and practical effects can be discerned
and used efficaciously.

CHAPTER VIII

THE NICENE CREED: ITS NATURE AND USE

In most Christian Liturgies, the Creed is preceeded by
the ascription: "Wisdom! Stand up! Hear ye the Symbol of our
holy Faith." This ascription points out, for those who are
spiritually awakened, what the Creed truly is and what our
attitude towards it should be. The Nicene Creed contains both
the essence of the Christian Faith and the key principles and
truths of the holy Wisdom or Primordial Tradition. It tells
us, in symbols, what we can find for ourselves, experientially,
in the higher states of spiritual consciousness. It points
to the most important truths and principles concerning Reality,
both in man and in the world; concerning God, man, and nature,
the Divine Spark, the soul, the Church, and evolution; it tells
us about what we are, why we are here, and what we shall become. As such, it deals with the most important questions man
can ask about himself and Reality and it is, indeed, Wisdom in
its true meaning: a symbolic blue-print of God, Humanity,
Creation, and their interrelationship. Moreover, by reaffirming
these essential truths, the devotee finds a way to:

a. Focus and bring to his awareness what is most important
    for him and for his life.

b. Stimulate the higher states of consciousness wherein these
    truths and principles will be experientially realized and
    lived.

c. Consciously cooperate with the realization and completion
    of God's Plan for man.

"Stand up" does not only mean to stand up physically (which,
by the way, is the central position, both in the Mystery Schools
and in the Orthodox Church, for approaching the Spiritual Powers
and opening one's self as fully as possible to the inrushing
Light) but also to wake up psychospiritually. It means, in
other words, to become conscious that one is engaging in a very
important task, to fully concentrate upon it, and to open one's
whole being (Tree of Life) to it.

"Hear the Symbol of our holy Faith" shows explicitly
that the Creed is written in symbolic and analogical language
rather than in descriptive and analytical language, and that it
contains the kernel of "our Faith," i.e. the key principles
and truths of the holy Wisdom.

Text of the Prayer:

"I believe in One God the Father Almighty,Maker of
heaven and earth and of all things visible and invisible.
    And in one Lord Jesus Christ, the only begotten Son of
God; Begotten of His Father, before all ages, Light of Light;
Very God of Very God; Begotten not made; Being of one essence
with the Father: By Whom all things were made. Who for us
men and for our salvation came down from heaven, and was incarnate by the Holy Ghost and of the Virgin Mary. And became
Man.
    And was crucified also for us under Pontius Pilate; He
suffered and was buried.
    And the third day He rose again according to the Scriptures.
    And ascended into heaven and sitteth on the right hand
of the Father.
    And He shall come again, with glory to judge both the
quick and the dead; Whose Kingdom shall have no end.
    And in the Holy Ghost, the Lord, the Giver of Life: Who
proceedeth from the Father: Who with the Father and the Son
together is worshipped and glorified: Who spake by the Prophets.
    And in One Holy Catholic and Apostolic Church.
    I acknowledge one baptism for the remission of sins.
    I look for the resurrection of the dead.
    And the life of the ages to come. Amen."

1. "I believe in One God the Father Almighty, Maker of heaven
    and earth and of all things visible and invisible." This
    statement declares and reaffirms, i.e. re-awakens inwardly,
    the belief in and for the Initiate, the experience of the
    Cosmic God, the Infinite Ocean of Light Who brought all
    Planes of Creation into being, the spiritual as well as the
    physical, the visible and the invisible. By re-awakening
    our belief in (and experience of) the Cosmic God, we auto-
    matically enter "in rapport" with Him and extend our con-
    sciousness towards Him, thus linking our being and conscious-
    ness to the whole of Reality and its ultimate Source and
    Essence.

2. "And in one Lord, Jesus Christ, the only begotten Son of
    God; Begotten of His Father, before all ages, Light of
    Light; Very God of Very God; Begotten not made; being of
    one essence with the Father: By Whom all things were made."
    This statement, as most religious statements, has a hieratic
    or double meaning: one for the normal, uninitiated man, the
    other for the spiritually awakened man, for the Initiate.

In the world, in history, it claims that Jesus Christ is the One Lord, the Son of God who is One with the Father. In man, in the microcosm, for the Initiate, it shows the nature of the Divine Spark that is our true Self. Our Divine Spark should be our Lord and Ruler, the integrating and unifying principle of our psyche and actions. It is the Divine Spark which is the only begotten Son of God, i.e. unlike our vehicles of expression (spiritual, mental, emotional, and physical) which are created or fashioned by the Divine Spark from the substance and energy of each Plane, the Divine Spark is "begotten" or emanated from the Divine Spirit. It existed long before the world or man's bodies, matter and energy, time and space, came into being. The Divine Spark is also essentially spiritual Light, Fire, and Life, an integral part of the Infinite Ocean of Life that manifests the Spirit. It is, therefore, divine in its origin and an integral part of the Spirit which made all things. By thinking about the Divine Spark and Its attributes, the devotee also attunes himself to It and becomes more receptive to Its being and eventually, as his consciousness expands and his life changes, he comes to the point where he can experience the reality and life of the Divine Spark within his own being and thus "existentially" experience the foregoing truths. In short, this passage helps the devotee to enter "in rapport" with his spiritual Self.

3. "Who for us men and for our salvation came down from heaven, and was incarnate by the Holy Ghost and the Virgin Mary. And became Man." This statement continues the development that was started with the previous one. On the exoteric level, it tells us about the historical Jesus the Christ and His Mission: that Christ came down from the spiritual worlds to make possible our salvation; that He was fathered by the Holy Ghost and born of the Theotokus, and that He became Man. On the esoteric level, however, it tells us more about our Divine Spark: that It came from the spiritual worlds and slowly involved into our vehicles where It now lies asleep; that It will be born into our souls, into our human consciousness, which will then experience the dawning of true spiritual consciousness by the power of the Holy Spirit; and that It will finally live in us and manifest Its Attributes and Will through our bodies, or vehicles, as It did in the God-Man Jesus Christ, Who is our prototype and archetype.

4. "And was crucified also for us under Pontius Pilate; He suffered and was buried." Jesus the Christ was crucified in the reign of Pontius Pilate. Like other men, He suffered, but He knew why He suffered and was buried. The Divine Spark in us is also crucified on the Cross of Matter: the present level of development and coordination of our bodies and our present state of consciousness does not enable It to express

Itself any more than our present social and public consciousness enable a truly inspired man to speak and to
act according to the dictates of his higher consciousness
and thus "crucify Him." The Divine Spark is thus buried,
entombed, and emprisoned in all of us and It "suffers"
as It cannot express Itself and manifest Its Will and
Attributes through our human temple.

5. "And the third day He rose again according to the Scriptures."
Exoterically, in the world, Jesus the Christ resurrected,
came to life again and left the tomb in the rock where His
body was lain. Such is what the New Testament tells us.
Esoterically, however, in ourselves, in our Tree of Life,
the Divine Spark and true spiritual consciousness will also
be resurrected; they will come to life again and permeate
our whole human consciousness when the "third day" (i.e.
genuine spiritual evolution as distinguished from animal
and biological evolution, the "first day" or phase, and
from human or psychosocial evolution, the "second day" or
phase) will begin. Such is what the unwritten Holy Tradition, or Hagia Sophia, tells us.

6. "And ascended into heaven and sitteth on the right hand of
the Father." Exoterically, we are told by the New Testament
that Jesus Christ ascended into heaven and is now "sitting"
on the right hand of the Father. Esoterically, when the
Divine Spark has indrawn into our soul, or invisible bodies,
and when spiritual consciousness has dawned, It will link us
up consciously with the Universal Spirit, the Father, and
with Cosmic Consciousness, the Kingdom of Heaven, which are
our true home and state of consciousness. In other words,
when a breakthrough of the superconscious into the conscious
occurs, Something (i.e. spiritual Light, Fire, and Life)
flows down into the center of our being and consciousness.
But when, It reascends whence It came, into the superconscious, It will this time elevate our whole being with
It and bring the very center of our consciousness and being
into the superconscious or spiritual realms.

7. "And He shall come again, with glory to judge both the quick
and the dead; Whose Kingdom shall have no end." Exoterically,
the Scriptures and the tradition of the Church tell us that
Jesus Christ will come again during the famous "Judgment Day"
to judge all those who are alive and those who are "dead"!
And that from this point onwards, the Millenium will be here
and that His Kingdom shall have no end. Esoterically, however, this statement refers again to the Divine Spark in us
and to spiritual consciousness. Spiritual consciousness
first appears in a flash and then disappears to reappear
when we least expect It. Eventually, however, It will come
back with spiritual Light that will surround our being (with
glory). Then, through the perspective of a heightened

spiritual consciousness, we shall look upon all of our
actions, words, and decisions, both past and present, in
quite a different light than we do in a normal state of
consciousness, and we shall evaluate them differently
than we do in our normal state of consciousness. It is
not an outside God or Power who will judge us, and our
lives, words, deeds, but our very own Higher Self, taking
the true love of God and of our fellow-men, and spiritual
growth and progress, as Its yardstick. The "quick and the
dead" here can be seen as meaning basically two things:
the things we did and that we remember and the things we
did but do not remember, and the things we did when we were
illuminated by spiritual consciousness as well as the things
we did in our normal state of consciousness.

"Whose Kingdom shall have no end." When the Divine Spark
takes control of our being and of our life, and when spiritual consciousness illuminates our stream of awareness, two
things happen:

a. One ceases to live in the past and in the future to live
    fully in the present, one steps outside the track and
    prison of time to enter the eternal Now.

b. One acquires conscious immortality or a continuity of
    consciousness which is no longer broken by cycles of
    birth and death, sleep and waking, and the rapidly
    narrowing and vanishing band of memory.

8. "And in the Holy Ghost, the Lord, the Giver of Life: Who
    proceedeth from the Father: Who with the Father and the Son
    together is worshipped and glorified: Who spake by the
    Prophets." Exoterically, this passage affirms our belief
    in the Third Person of the Holy Trinity, the Holy Spirit,
    Who is the Spirit of Truth, the Giver and Ruler of Life,
    Who proceeds from the Father and is bestowed by the Son
    and Who, with Them, should be worshipped and glorified.
    Finally, it asserts that it is the same Spirit of Truth who
    inspired and spoke through the countless genuine Prophets
    of humanity.

    Esoterically, by affirming the reality of the Holy Spirit
    and by directing our focused attention to It, this formula
    "tunes us in" to the Presence and Power of the Holy Spirit,
    and develops a psychic channel through which It can now
    manifest and work through our human consciousness. The
    Holy Spirit is one aspect, or manifestation, of the Univer-
    sal Spirit or Divine Light. The Universal Spirit, or Divine
    Light, is One in essence but Three in expression. This
    specific expression of the Universal Spirit is the "Giver
    of Life," the Power that quickens, energizes, and enlivens
    all It comes in contact with. On the Tree of Life, the
    Center through which It manifests is Binah in the macrocosm

and Yesod in the microcosm. It is Divine Wisdom and Divine
Love that beget Divine Life and Divine Creative Energy.
First, we had the religion of the Father through Jehova,
then we had the religion of the Son through Jesus Christ,
but now it is the religion of the Holy Spirit that we shall
develop and which Jesus promised to us as His greatest Gift.
While the religion of the Father and of the Son was essentially a "faith religion," i.e. a non-experiential religion
without the personal experience and realization of its
truths and tenets, the religion of the Holy Spirit, which
is in the process of being born, will be, essentially, an
experiential one--one in which the individual will have a
direct and first-hand experience and a personal realization
of the truths and promises symbolically represented by the
former. The coming religion of the Holy Spirit, in other
words, will be a Path of Initiation, leading its devotees to
genuine spiritual Illumination, which has been foreshadowed
and promised by the former. For it is through the quickening
and life-giving power of the Holy Spirit that the Tree of Life
is lit up, that key psychospiritual Centers are activated
therein, and that the higher states of consciousness are
brought through.

Like the Power and the Center of the Father and of the Son,
so the Power and the Centers of the Holy Spirit have to be
"filled with Light," activated, and brought into proper
function into the Sphere of Sensation. Then, as the Holy
Spirit inspired and spoke through Prophets, Initiates, and
Adepts of old, so It will now generate a breakthrough of the
superconscious into the conscious and It will inspire and
speak through us.

9. "And in One Holy Catholic and Apostolic Church." Esoter-
    ically speaking, this affirmation can be interpreted in
    quite a different fashion than in its exoteric version.
    There is, indeed, One Church or Religion that is truly holy,
    i.e. whole and complete, that is truly catholic, i.e. uni-
    versal, and of which Apostolic Christianity was an external
    and symbolic representation on earth. But this Holy and
    Catholic Religion, that has existed from the first appearance
    of man on earth and which will remain with us till humanity
    has completed its earthly evolution, has never been in-
    stitutionalized and fully incarnated on earth and never will
    be. For it is the One Source and Trunk from which all organ-
    ized religions have drawn their deepest insights and their
    loftiest truths, and always will, but which they will never
    be able to "monopolize" and to express more than partially
    and in some of its aspects. This Religion is no more and
    no less than the Inner Church, the Church Triumphant, the
    Communion of Saints, the true Brotherhood of the Rosy-Cross,
    or the Assembly of the Adepts of the Spirit. Its deepest

sanctuaries on earth are the <u>hearts</u> and the <u>human con-
sciousness</u> of the true Mystics and Initiates who walk the
earth. Its symbols and external manifestations, however,
can be found in <u>all</u> the great world religions. This
Religion is the true and living repository of the Primordial Tradition or the Hagia Sophia. Its major symbol or
image is that given by Jesus when He said to Peter: "And
thou art Peter, and on this rock I shall build My Church."
Peter when asked by Jesus "Who am I" has answered "Thou art
the Christ, the Son of the Living God." What transpired
here is the following: it was the Divine Spark in Peter
which enabled him to recognize the Divine Spark, or Divinity, or Jesus. Jesus, in turn, affirmed that His Living
Church would be made up of all those human beings in whom
the Divine Spark had been awakened and who, via a breakthrough of the superconscious into the conscious, can
recognize the Living God in others and in the world, that
is, of true Initiates and spiritually awakened human beings

10. "I acknowledge one baptism for the remission of sins."
Exoterically, this passage means that only the "Baptism"
of the Christian Faith and, sometimes, of even only one
Christian Church is valid to wash away one's sins!
Esoterically, however, there is but one "Baptism" or openin
of a key psychospiritual Center, purification of the Aura,
and transformation of human consciousness through the opening of a channel by which spiritual Energies can flow into
our psyche, and that is the down-pouring of spiritual Light
in response to a deep need of the human heart when man is
ready for it.

11. "I look for the resurrection of the dead." Exoterically,
this was interpreted to mean that those who had died would
"come back to life" or "be resurrected" at the legendary
"Final Judgment." Esoterically, it has several meanings.
The most important of which are:

a. That the many faculties and spiritual powers of man
which are presently dormant or inactive will be "awaken
and activated by the quickening power of the Spirit.

b. That many of the things which we have done, said, and
experienced but forgotten, will be remembered and broug
to consciousness again when spiritual consciousness
will illuminate us.

c. That eventually man will acquire spiritual consciousnes
Life Eternal, or conscious immortality and thus be
"resurrected" from the "dead." This "resurrection,"
moreover, will take place at different points in different degrees in one's spiritual evolution. It does
take place, to a certain extent, when we pass on to the
"other side" and when we pray with great fervor, or

consciously receive the Sacraments. Its fullest and
highest form, however, will take place at the time of our
spiritual Initiation.

12. "And the life of the ages to come." Exoterically, this
meant that man's consciousness does not perish at death and
still lives on. Esoterically, it continues and completes
the foregoing statement, pointing to the fact that man will
continue his spiritual evolution and eventually attain conscious immortality, or Life Eternal.

CHAPTER IX

THE BEATITUDES: THEIR NATURE AND USE

The Beatitudes is another very important document which
constitutes a major pillar of the theoretical and practical
training of the Western Spiritual Tradition. As a whole, the
Beatitudes contain a blue-print of man's conscious spiritual
evolution and of how he may deliberately enter the Path of
genuine self-actualization and Self-realization through graded
steps. As such, they can be used for concentration, meditation,
and contemplation exercises, for theurgic work, and for establishing a vital link between the conscious and the superconscious.

Text of the Prayer:

"Blessed are the poor in spirit: for theirs is the
Kingdom of Heaven.
Blessed are they that mourn: for they shall be comforted.
Blessed are the meek: for they shall inherit the earth.
Blessed are they which do hunger and thirst after right-
eousness: for they shall be filled.
Blessed are the merciful: for they shall obtain mercy.
Blessed are the pure in heart: for they shall see God.
Blessed are the peacemakers: for they shall be called
the children of God.
Blessed are they which are persecuted for righteousness
sake: for theirs is the Kingdom of Heaven.
Blessed are ye, when men shall revile you, and shall say
all manner of evil against you falsely, for My sake. Rejoice and
be exceedingly glad; for great is your reward in heaven."

1. "Blessed are the poor in spirit: for theirs is the Kingdom
   of Heaven." This formula, sung or recited antiphonically,
   represents, as do later ones, the dialogue between the
   Higher Self and the lower self and, in so doing, it blazes
   open a psychic channel between the superconscious and the
   conscious.

   a. To bless means to establish a consciousness and energy
      channel whereby higher energies and vibrations can flow
      into the lower ones and whereby the lower ones can tune
      into higher ones.

b. To be poor in spirit means, here, to feel a lack and, therefore, a desire for something that one feels is very important.

c. The Kingdom of Heaven is the higher state of consciousness in which spiritual consciousness is operating and wherein one experiences one's true Self, God's Wisdom and Love, and the goodness of Creation.

This affirmation, therefore, means: those who feel a great lack and desire for spiritual things, which are seen as being very important, will eventually be blessed by the Divine Spark as they seek them. A channel or "ladder of Jacob" is then established between the conscious and the superconscious. Through this channel, higher energies and consciousness will flow into one's human consciousness eventually flooding it with Light and awakening true spiritual consciousness therein.

2. "Blessed are they that mourn: for they shall be comforted." "They that mourn" are those that are seeking what they feel is very important for them, which they feel they are lacking but which they desire intensely.

"They shall be comforted" means that, eventually, they will find that which they seek: they will be "blessed" by the Divine Spark and will attain spiritual consciousness which is the Kingdom of Heaven.

The second affirmation, therefore, tells us that, to achieve Illumination and spiritual consciousness, one must "mourn" for it, i.e. desire it intensely, involve one's emotions with it which will bring down "blessings" from the Divine Spark and, eventually, Illumination, which is the only thing that can bring true and lasting comfort to a human being. As such, this affirmation reinforces and continues the operation of the first.

3. "Blessed are the meek: for they shall inherit the earth." The key symbols here are: blessed, the meek, and the earth.

We have already discussed the esoteric meaning of the word "to bless," which is to transfer consciousness and life from a higher source to a lower one.

"The meek," esoterically speaking, are neither those who are passive, timid, or cowardly, nor those who will not fight for their self-respect and rights. Rather, in this context, the "meek" indicate those who are open, receptive to the Light, and to the flow of inspiration and intuition coming down from "above" and who will not "block it off" or resist it.

"The earth" refers, on the one hand, to man's normal state of consciousness and, on the other hand, to man's physical body and to his "little Kingdom" or personality.

The whole formula, therefore, means, esoterically, that those who are open and receptive to the Light and the higher inspiration, who do not "drown it out," or "struggle against" the Will of God, of the Divine Spark within, will "inherit the earth," i.e. achieve a psychosynthesis around the center of their higher Self and acquire self-mastery, which is one of the major objectives of all true spiritual training. It also points to the fact that there is a time in life to face whatever forces confront us and a time to bend to them so as to husband one's resources to be used again at a later time; for the tree that bends to the wind will not be broken while the tree that cannot bend might be uprooted.

4. "Blessed are they which do hunger and thirst after righteousness: for they shall be filled." This formula reminds us that those who seek will eventually find what they are seeking, irrespective of how long and hard the search might be; it also reminds us that we must desire righteousness, i.e. what is right, the Will of the Divine in us, as much as we can hunger and thirst for food and water, if we are to make true spiritual progress. Finally, it tells us that to be filled with Divine Light, to flood our stream of awareness with spiritual energies, we must desire them and hunger for them with all our heart and soul.

5. "Blessed are the merciful: for they shall obtain mercy." This affirmation, whose central symbol is mercy, can be esoterically interpreted from two basic standpoints: that of the microcosm and that of the macrocosm. From the standpoint of the macrocosm, it points to man's relationship with the world and shows, essentially, that as man treats others, so he will be treated by them; that if he shows mercy, i.e. tolerance, understanding, and compassion towards others, so they, in turn, will show mercy towards him. Underpinning this relationship stands the law of Cause and Effect, the law of Action and Reaction or what is known esoterically as the law of Karma.

From the standpoint of the microcosm, it points to the relationship of man's conscious with the superconscious. Mercy is the title and key attribute of Chesed, and Chesed is the highest of man's "existential Sephiroth," or psychospiritual Centers, which connects him with the Supernals. Underpinning this relationship is the law of "like attracts like" and that, in order to make "Gold" one must have "Gold." As man cultivates and expresses mercy, i.e. tolerance, understanding, and compassion in his human way and daily life, so higher spiritual Energies will flow from the superconscious into his consciousness. As man gives to his fellow-men, so he will receive from the Divine Spark; as man treats his fellow-men on the horizontal dimension, so will his inner psychic structure enable his Divine Spark to deal with him.

6. "Blessed are the pure in heart: for they shall see God."
    The "pure in heart" has, understandably, several meanings
    and correspondences on several levels of consciousness.
    The major ones, for our present purposes, are:

    a. To have a Heart Center that is cleansed, awakened, and
        balanced.

    b. To have an Aura, or Sphere of Sensation, that has been
        cleansed, balanced, and spiritualized by the Light of
        God.

    c. To have noble, pure, elevating emotions, desires, and
        aspirations, i.e. to love and to yearn after the Divine
        Light, justice, goodness, and wholesomeness.

    To "see God" can also have several meanings, chief of which
    are:

    a. To become aware of and experience the Divine Presence, the
        Life of the Divine Spark.

    b. To feel the Divine Light rushing into our Sphere of Sen-
        sation and quickening the whole field of human conscious-
        ness.

    c. To see the Divine Light in ourselves and in others as
        our Divine Spark becomes conscious of Itself in our
        human Temple.

    This formula, therefore, is designed to guide man to examine,
    purify, and raise his motives, intentions, and aspirations
    so that by purifying his emotions and intentions, he may
    enable the Divine Light to flow into him, to reveal Its Will
    to him, and to quicken him into a new and higher state of
    consciousness.

7. "Blessed are the peacemakers: for they shall be called the
    children of God." Here the key symbols are: peacemakers and
    children of God.

    "Peacemakers" can again be interpreted horizontally, in the
    world, and vertically, in man. Horizontally, a "peacemaker"
    is one who helps to settle conflicts and disputes between
    human beings, who brings about social peace or social inte-
    gration.

    Vertically, a "peacemaker" is one who brings peace or harmony
    in his own psyche, i.e. one who strives to achieve his own
    psychosynthesis. It is also one who works to harmonize his
    human faculties with the Divine Will and Life in him, i.e. one
    who strives for union with God, or spiritual psychosynthesis.

As a whole, this formula points to the fact that those who strive for peace, for personal, interpersonal, and transpersonal psychosynthesis will be "blessed," i.e. receive an outpouring of Divine Light from the Divine Spark.

8. "Blessed are they which are persecuted for righteousness sake: for theirs is the Kingdom of Heaven." To be "persecuted for righteousness sake" means to be willing to suffer, to undergo hardships, and persecutions for the sake of doing what one knows to be right. It requires, moreover, a great deal of Faith and of conviction in what one knows to be right. Finally, it demands a great effort of the will which further develops and strengthens the will. Unless man has the courage and the strength to fight and to suffer for his convictions, for what he believes to be right, he is not ready for and will not be able to implement the promptings of his Divine Spark and higher conscience. This set of faculties, faith, courage, conviction, and will-power must be developed on the Path before one can reach true Illumination. Once they are developed, however, and when one is willing and able to follow the dictates of one's higher conscience regardless of the personal implications these have for one's social and material well-being in the world, one will find oneself well on the way to spiritual Illumination.

Two important "hints" of this formula are:

a. That, in order to "speed up" one's evolution and pay one's Karmic debts, as one is treading the Path of spiritual growth, all kinds of afflictions, persecutions, and trials are likely to befall the candidate.

b. That society and social conscience being what they are, it is hardly possible to live in this world and obey the dictates of one's higher conscience, rather than those of society, without being misunderstood and persecuted. But, for those who are spiritually enlightened, even these persecutions and afflictions have their raison d'etre and perform a useful function in God's Plan.

9. "Blessed are ye, when men shall revile you, and shall say all manner of evil against you falsely for my sake. Rejoice and be exceedingly glad; for great is your reward in heaven." As hinted in the previous explanation, when a candidate enters the spiritual Path and begins to tread it firmly, he leaves the large and winding road of evolution that most human beings travel on for a much narrower and steeper Path wherein he will meet fewer souls. In so doing two basic things can be expected:

a. He will have trials, tests, hardships, and tribu-
   lations that will seem to fall upon him from all
   sides. He will compress in a few months and years
   the experiences and lessons he would normally have
   undergone over a much longer period of time. He
   will greatly accelerate the paying up of past Karma
   and will be tempted and tested much beyond what
   most men and women are. As an old saying rightfully
   puts it: "laugh and the world will laugh with you;
   cry, and you will cry alone."

b. His values, frame of reference, and basic principles
   will change noticeably, first in his human consciousness and then in his overt behavior. Rather than living by the values and dictates of his society, of what
   is politic and expedient, rather than pleasing his
   superiors or public opinion, he will do what his conscience, what the voice of his higher Self prompts
   him to do regardless of personal and social consequences.
   Naturally, in so doing, he will incur the displeasure,
   the misunderstanding, and the persecutions of many.

If, indeed, it is the voice of his higher conscience, of
his Divine Spark, the Christ-within, and not the voice of
his pride, of his reason, or of some other subconscious
or sociocultural entity he is following and suffering for,
two things will normally ensue:

a. He will greatly strengthen and further develop his
   faith, his determination, and his will-power thereby
   and thus unfold valuable psychospiritual faculties.

b. Once his tests and ordeals in the world are over, he will
   rapidly expand his consciousness, unfold spiritual
   consciousness, and obtain his "reward" or the fruits
   of the Great Work in the higher states of consciousness
   (in Heaven), i.e. the bliss and ecstasy of being consciously linked with the Source and Essence of all
   Wisdom, Love, and Life.

It is well known that society, the collective conscience
of a group, fears and attacks the unfamiliar--those who
do not conform to its standards and norms. Thus, two op-
posite types of "deviants" are always persecuted and re-
viled, i.e. outcast by society: those who are further
ahead in evolution, the Saints and spiritually enlightened
human beings and those who are behind in evolution, the
criminals, the idiots, and the insane.

This document, therefore, clearly outlines the work and prepares the candidate to enter into and walk upon the Path of spiritual Initiation, the attainment of self-actualization and Self-realization. As such, it should be used often as a treasure house of symbols for meditation and for theurgic purposes, and to have a set of well-established guide lines by which to interpret many daily events and the results of one's aspirations and work.

CHAPTER X

THE HAIL MARY: ITS NATURE AND USE

In many of the old liturgies, and particularly in the liturgies of the Orthodox Church, the Hail Mary was formulated as follows:

Text of the Prayer:

"The Mother of the Lord and Light-giver, let us exalt: Hail O Birth-giver Mary, full of grace, the Lord is with Thee. Blessed are Thou amongst women and blessed is the fruit of Thy womb. For Thou hast borne the Savior of our Souls."

This prayer, short and simple as it is, is one of the "Seven Fundamentals." Thus it is a most important spiritual document containing profound esoteric knowledge and a series of integrated and practical exercises designed to establish a breakthrough between the conscious and the superconscious, to fill the human Aura with spiritual Light, and to harmonize man's human self with his spiritual Self.

1.   The "Mother of the Lord and Light-giver" is, in man, his own soul, his Tree of Life and Aura, whence the Light flows and which must, someday, become the "birth-giver" or matrix for the Christ-consciousness. In the world, it is the Anima Mundi, the soul of the world, or the earth's collective psychic atmosphere. In history, Mary, the mother of the Master Jesus, became the archetype, or perfect symbol and personification, of the human soul and of the Anima Mundi. She was an advanced Initiate who became the earthly mother of the man in whom the Christ Spirit would incarnate fully and consciously. Mary, therefore, represents the ideal woman, the perfection of the female principle, and the incarnation of the eternal feminine-- a part of which we all have within our being. To exhalt the "Light-giver" is to focus all our attention upon the soul and the Tree of Life, to raise its vibratory rate and to heighten our state of consciousne, so that it will, indeed, become a light and life-giver, the seat of the Christ consciousness for ourselves and for the world.

2.   "Hail O Birth-giver Mary, full of grace, the Lord is with Thee." This exercise contains one of the most important and powerful spiritual exercises that man can use to fill

93

his soul with Light, to raise his vibratory level, and to expand his consciousness. As with all other spiritual exercises, it demands Faith to make it "operational," i.e. a great deal of concentration, visualization, and some understanding of what one is doing and why, and a profound love for God and for the Great Work.

By saying "Hail O Birth-giver Mary," the candidate focuses all his attention and consciousness upon his soul, reminding himself (and then experiencing it, if possible) that his soul is the "Birth-giver" or matrix for human consciousness on all planes and levels, and that it is in his Tree of Life that, for him, God, Man, and Nature are "born," i.e. spring forth into consciousness.

By adding "full of grace," the candidate now visualizes and experiences the Divine Light slowly filling his entire Aura, activating his Tree of Life, and suffusing his whole consciousness. When performed with the utmost Faith, and when the candidate is ready for it, this is one of the key exercises that will bring about the "Golden Dawn" of spiritual consciousness, the slow awakening of a higher and qualitatively different state of consciousness in man.

By concluding "the Lord is with Thee," the candidate affirms and should experience, if possible, that, once the soul, the Tree of Life and Aura, have been purified and consecrated by the Divine Light, and once they have been vitalized and filled with the same Light, the Divine Spark is now operating through it, the spiritual Self is in it and manifests Its Energies and Attributes through it.

This operation, in a nutshell, contains and represents the Great Work in its essence and the ultimate realization that all human beings must eventually come to: the union of God with man, of the spiritual Self with the psyche so that human consciousness can now manifest and reflect the Spirit in the world.

By stating this fact and "prophecy," one does not realize it immediately but one builds a thought-form and establishes the ground-work, the attitude and state of consciousness which will eventually lead to its full realization. One thing is a symbolic representation of something (say a map of a country or a film showing some of its landscape) and another is its realization (being in the country and seeing the landscape with one's own eyes). Ideas and thought-forms,however, have a peculiar property: they are a self-fulfilling prophecy, they contain an inner energy and dynamic which drives man, both subconsciously and superconsciously, to realize and objectify them in the world.

3. "Blessed art Thou amongst women and blessed is the fruit of Thy womb." Exoterically, this formula, so often used by Christian Churches, meant that Mary was more blessed and pure than any other woman and that the fruit of her womb, Jesus, was also especially blessed in that He was the Son of God rather than the son of man. This would make Mary a "special darling of God" which would represent an injustice and an arbitrariness on the part of God. This, of course, is not and cannot be so. Its true meaning, however, as with so many prayers, rituals, and spiritual documents, can only be discovered at the esoteric level, when we translate and interpret these wonderful symbols, archetypes, and analogies in terms of their correspondences in the microcosm. To take them literally is foolishness and hides even further the great treasure they contain--without even searching for it. All human beings and all souls will be blessed in due time, when they are ready for it, when they ask for it, and to the extent that they can receive and handle a true blessing.

"Blessed amongst women" means two things, or one thing on two different levels:

a. That the woman, or human being, who succeeds in establishing a breakthrough or conscious contact with the Divine Spark will, indeed, be "blessed" amongst women or other human beings. "Blessed" here means experiencing a transfer of life, energy, and consciousness from a higher source to a lower one, from the spiritual Self into the human self and its vehicle of expression, the psyche.

b. That the feminine principle which succeeds in establishing a contact and rapport with the Divine Spark will, likewise, be "blessed" and enlivened.

"Blessed is the fruit of Thy womb" means that the being or principle to which the woman is giving birth is also "blessed."

Every woman and every feminine principle, which woman embodies, must give birth to some "being" or principle. Love, if it is genuine, must and will bear fruit, but this "fruit" can appear on different planes of being. It can be a child on the physical plane, but it can also be a feeling, an idea, an intuition, a new insight, realization, or state of consciousness. A female principle without love will remain barren and a barren female principle always remains an unfulfilled female principle. Whatever is born always reflects the nature and origin of the male and female principles which gave birth to it, the "force" and the "form" which engendered it.

In this case, what is born, the "fruit," is spiritual
consciousness which is engendered by the spiritual
Self and the psyche, which is thus in contact with the
Divine Spark which blesses Its offspring in human consciousness.

4. "For Thou hast borne the Savior of our souls." This
affirmation further reinforces and completes the pre-
ceding one. Exoterically, the Savior of our souls is
Jesus the Christ; esoterically, it is the Divine Spark
which engenders true spiritual consciousness in the
Tree of Life and the human Aura. Thus the last and
completing formula concludes the whole operation. At
this point, the candidate should feel and experience
that his soul is filled with Divine Light and Life,
that spiritual consciousness is in direct contact with
the spiritual Self, and that It alone is the Savior,
i.e. the unifying and life-giving principle of his
being and consciousness.

To show the universality, manifold correspondences and
varied analogical implications and possibilities of this
spiritual document, I shall now look at, analyze, and interpret it through the perspective and vocabulary of psychosynthesis, which is the latest and most advanced of the approaches
of the modern human and social sciences.

1. "Hail O Birth-giver Mary, full of grace, the Lord is with
Thee." This ascription can be interpreted here, as the
student turns all of his attention and consciousness
towards his psyche and its functions, as his seeing them
and sensing them being filled with the life and energies
of the spiritual Self which harmonizes and integrates them
into a true personal psychosynthesis. At a latter and
more advanced level, it means to actually experience and
live this personal psychosynthesis.

2. "Blessed art Thou amongst women and blessed is the fruit
of Thy womb" can be interpreted as an inrushing stream
of intuition and inspiration flowing from the spiritual
Self and the superconscious into the field of consciousness, the human self, and the 7 functions of the psyche,
as an unbroken and two-way stream. The student must first
visualize and then feel and experience this process taking
place within himself.

3. "For Thou hast borne the Savior of our souls" means here
the recognition that the final unfoldment, coordination,
and integration of all of man's faculties can only come
about through a spiritual psychosynthesis. At a later
and more advanced stage, the student must have an actual
personal experience of that spiritual psychosynthesis

whereby the spiritual Self can now flow into and become the "human self" of man and express Its attributes
through the 7 functions of man's psyche in his life
and in the world.

Here the perspective, the terminology, is different but
the fundamental principles and truths depicted by this spiritual document remain the same for anyone (or any system)
who has truly decoded and penetrated into its central core,
and who has had a direct personal experience of it.

CHAPTER XI

THE TEN COMMANDMENTS: THEIR NATURE AND USE

To understand the deeper nature, the many correspondences, the philosophical and ethical implications, and the
practical applications of the Ten Commandments, we must
first turn to their exoteric and historical meaning--for the
path to the esoteric depths and mysteries always begins with
the outer, the exoteric, or the "letter" of the teachings.
This, incidentally, is the reason why, generally, before
one can begin to ascend towards the heights of the Spirit and
the descent towards the depths of the unconscious, one must
have memorized and mastered the outer, surface levels, or the
"letter" of spiritual teachings. Both world religions and the
true Mystery Schools acknowledge this principle and require
it of their devotees and students.

Let us begin, therefore, by briefly looking at the
historical and traditional circumstances through which the
Ten Commandments were given to humanity, for many deeper or
esoteric secrets concerning their nature and application are
contained therein for those who have "eyes to see" and "ears
to hear." Then we shall proceed to look at their orthodox
or "literal" interpretation and at the major sociocultural
impact they had, as an ethical system, upon Western civilization. Finally, after this necessary preamble, we shall turn
to the gist of our analysis, to an in-depth and detailed study
of their "esoteric" or spirituals meanings, correspondences,
and applications. Again, let the serious and mature student
bear in mind that the true "esoteric" and "spiritual secrets"
and teachings, that the deepest living wisdom of mankind,
cannot be found in some "occult school" or "esoteric doctrine"
but, rather, in the well-known though generally little understood teachings and symbols of the great world religions, and
throughout the world of nature which we can behold every day;
moreover, that these "arcane principles and mysteries" are not
so much to be grasped and discussed intellectually as they are
to be lived and experienced, in the depths and heights of one's
being, in one's daily life. This is why "serious and mature
students" are one thing and "curiosity seekers" another, and
why genuine schools and orders are continually seeking to
discriminate between the former and the latter.

98

I. Historical circumstances and traditional explanation given
by the Bible and the Judeo-Christian traditions for the Ten
Commandments.

In the Bible, we can find the following account of
how the Ten Commandments were given to mankind:

"In the third month after the departure of the children
of Israel out of the land of Egypt. . . they came to
the wilderness of Sinai and the encampment in the wilderness; and there Israel camped before the mountain.
And Moses went up to God and God called him out of the
mountain and said to him. . . If you will obey my voice
indeed and keep my covenant, then shall you be my be-
loved ones above all peoples, for all the earth is mine. . .
And the Lord said to Moses, Lo, I am coming to you in a
thick cloud, that the people may hear when I speak with
you and also believe you forever. . . And it came to pass
on the third day in the morning that there were thunders
and lightenings, and a thick cloud appeared on the
mountain. . . And the whole mountain of Sinai was smoking
because the Lord descended upon it in fire; and the smoke
thereof ascended like the smoke of a furnace, and the
whole mountain quaked greatly. And when the blast of the
trumpted sounded long and grew louder and louder, Moses
spoke and God answered him by voice. And the Lord came
down upon mount Sinai; to the very top of the mountain;
and the Lord called Moses up to the top of the mountain;
and Moses went up. . . And God spoke all these words saying
'I am the Lord your God, who brought you out of the land
of Egypt, out of the house of bondage. You shall have
no other Gods except me. You shall not make for yourself
any graven image, or any likeness of anything that is in
heaven above or that is in the earth beneath or that is
in the water under the earth. . . You shall not take a
false oath in the name of the Lord your God; for the
Lord will not declare him innocent who takes an oath in
his name falsely. Remember the Sabbath day to keep it
holy. Six days shall you labor and do your work; but the
seventh day is a sabbath to the Lord your God; in it you
shall not do any work. . . For in six days the Lord made
heaven and earth, the seas, and all things that are in
them, and rested on the seventh day. . . Honor your father
and your mother, that your days may be long upon the land
which the Lord your God gives you. You shall not kill.
You shall not commit adultery. You shall not covet your
neighbor's house. You shall not covet your neighbor's
wife. . . nor anything that is your neighbor's.' . . .
And all the people observed the thundering and the light-
ening flashes and the sound of the trumpet and the mountain
smoking and when the people saw all this, they were afraid
and stood far off. And the Lord said to Moses. . . an

altar of earth shall you make to me, and you shall sacrifice on it your burnt offerings and your peace offerings, your sheep and your oxen; in every place where I shall make a memorial to my name I will come to you and I will bless you." (Exodus 20. 1-24).

In essence, such are the Ten Commandments and how Moses received them.

II. The orthodox or "literal" interpretation of the Ten Commandments and the major sociocultural impact they had as an ethical system upon Western civilization.

The Ten Commandments, as given by Moses to the Israelites at the foot of mount Sinai, have generally been interpreted at a literal level, i.e. according to the historical and cultural definitions assigned to them by a given religion and by a given people who adopted them. Thus:

1. "I am the Lord thy God, thou shall have no other Gods before me" has been interpreted in two basic ways:

   a. Generally, it has meant that there is but one God for all human beings and not many Gods. This was the foundation of a monotheistic religion which established the "fatherhood of God" and the "brotherhood of man."

   b. Specifically, it meant that the one true God is that of one's religion (e.g. Jehovah, the Trinity, Jesus Christ and, later, the God of one's specific denomination).

2. "Thou shall make no idols of me" has been interpreted again in two basic ways:

   a. Generally, it has meant that no image, statue, or symbol ever devised by the human mind could ever represent God who is a formless Spirit. This even though the former could be used as aesthetic means to represent in a human form the formless spiritual reality.

   b. Specifically, it has also come to mean for inconoclasts and strict fundamentalists that religion should be stripped bare of all its artistic expressions and that God should be approached in austere external simplicity and through the naked will of one's inner consciousness.

3. "Thou shall not use the name of the Lord thy God in vain" has been interpreted to mean:

a.   That one should never utter the name of God lightly or as an exclamation.

b.   That one should never take an oath in the name of God, which has been taken literally by some radical groups.

4.   "Thou shall keep holy the day of the Lord thy God" has meant, generally, that one day a week, Saturday or Sunday, should be devoted to religious services and pursuits, and that one should neither work nor engage in worldly pursuits during that day (e.g. drinking, gambling, sex, theater, etc.).

5.   "Thou shall honor thy father and thy mother" has, generally, meant that one should obey and respect one's earthly parents.

6.   "Thou shall not kill" has, generally, meant that no man should take the life of another human being. . .except in time of war or for self-defense.

7.   "Thou shall not commit adultery" has, generally, meant that one could not have sexual relations with a woman or a man who is legally married to someone else. . . but it applied particularly to women as a double standard was widely practiced.

8.   "Thou shall not steal" has meant literally that one could not take something which belongs to another human being.

9.   "Thou shall not bear false witness" has, generally, meant two things:

a.   That one should not lie.

b.   That one should not defame or tell untruths about others.

10. "Thou shall not covet the wife or any of the possessions of thy neighbor" has meant that one should not desire to have, or to appropriate for oneself, what belongs to another human being but, rather, that one should "work" or "earn" one's possessions and privileges.

These Ten Commandments, in their various definitions and forms of interpretation which are very similar in essence, have provided the ethical cornerstone, the central core of all theoretical and practical ethical systems of the various western civilizations.   The very life and survival of a group, or nation, has depended largely upon them.   Moreover, their functional equivalents, with slight differences of wording and interpretation, can also be found in other religions and in the Eastern cults, whether in the Buddhist, Shintoist, Confusian, or Hindu systems. These commandments, therefore, in their exoteric interpretation, can be seen as constituting the core elements, or minimum ethical imperatives, necessary to enable a human society to function as a viable system and to endure through time.

Two central points can be made in terms of their exoteric interpretation:

a. That the Ten Commandments have essentially one basic meaning and interpretation, which are defined by the religious and social authorities of a given society and which are valid for all members of that society.

b. That this one basic meaning and interpretation, given by the Church and the state, deals essentially with man's attitudes and behavior patterns in the world, towards his church, his state, and his fellow-men.

III. The esoteric or spiritual interpretation of the Ten Commandments.

Just as we found two basic points characterizing the exoteric interpretation of the Ten Commandments so, now, we can establish three main points that characterize their esoteric interpretation.

a. The Ten Commandments are seen as an open symbolic system with many different meanings, interpretations, correspondences, and applications which change, expand, and broaden with our degree of maturity and experience in life and particularly with our state of consciousness. To different states of consciousness correspond different meanings, associations, and applications of the Ten Commandments.

b. The esoteric interpretation of the Ten Commandments focuses essentially upon an explanation and application of the Ten Commandments within man's "little kingdom," i.e. within man rather than in the world.

c. The esoteric or spiritual approach looks at the Ten Commandments not only as a set of ethical and philosophical guidelines to regulate human interaction but also as a set of practical spiritual exercises designed to bring about the completion and perfection of man, i.e. the unfoldment of spiritual consciousness through which these commandments can be truly understood and lived in one's daily life. Here, therefore, the Ten Commandments are not only philosophical principles and norms for social intercourse but also and especially exercises for self-actualization and Self-realization.

From the esoteric standpoint, the conditions under which the Ten Commandments were given to mankind are highly significant and indicative of their origin, nature, and application. The Ten Commandments were given to Moses on top of mount Sinai after a long period of wandering in the wilderness in quest of the promised land. It was God, the Lord or Divine Spark, who revealed them to Moses, the leader and most evolved Initiate of his nation, amidst light, fire, clouds, and smoke. Moses represents the prototype, the living exemplar, of the true Initiate of all times. Hence, it is not so much that we have to look up to Moses or follow his teachings as it is that we must become what he was, that we must realize and incarnate the paradigmatic model he gave us. Here Moses is also the symbol of the higher human consciousness a man can develop by his own efforts. Thus, esoterically speaking, this event refers to an inner experience that every human being can have and will eventually have. At this point, man's higher consciousness, obtained through his own efforts and experiences, must climb on the sacred Mountain of Consciousness towards the top where the superconscious resides with the Divine Spark. There the Lord (i.e. the spiritual consciousness of the Divine Spark) will descend towards it with a manifestation of Light and Fire and will reveal the Divine Laws ruling all creation (the Tree of Life on the Four Worlds: Aziluth, divine consciousness; Briah, the superconscious; Yetzirah, the conscious; and Assiah, the unconscious). The fog or smoke seen drawing a curtain between the top of the mountain where Moses climbs and the base of the mountain where the people reside symbolize the veil or curtain that separates the superconscious from normal consciousness.

All human beings, at a certain point of spiritual development, can and will have the experience that Moses had on mount Sinai. For the living laws of God and creation are buried deep within the higher reaches of human consciousness, and the Divine Spark in each of us will reveal them "in spirit and in truth" when we truly seek them and have prepared ourselves to receive them worthily, i.e. when we are ready and capable of putting them into practice and of "living" them. Moreover, as we expand and raise our consciousness and as we mature through experience on earth, we shall discover ever greater and deeper meanings, correspondences, and applications of these laws of which the Ten Commandments are the blue-print and the symbolic representation. The deeper meanings, correspondences, and the practical applications of the Ten Commandments will be revealed to us by the Divine Spark (through the power of the Holy Spirit as the Bible says) as we seek to live and to incarnate them in our being.

As an advanced student of the Mysteries put it:

"The Ten Commandments contain very specific theoretical
and practical information and exercises for the unfoldment of our psyche and of our spiritual powers--
which alone can, ultimately, satisfy the hunger of our
souls. . . The way to spiritual attainment goes through
a very long, steep, and dangerous path wherein Divine
Guidance is absolutely necessary. The central goal of
all spiritual development is and can only be <u>union with
God</u>. The attainment of all psychic and spiritual powers
are actually secondary to this great goal, a by-product
of it, as it were. One of the major means by which to
achieve this great goal is to live by God's Laws, to
incorporate the teachings of all world-saviors in our
mental and psychic being, to live them and exemplify
them--there is simply no substitute for this.

Prayer, and its living application in daily life, is also
invaluable to enable us to establish a direct personal
contact with the Higher Planes of Consciousness and Being.
The guidance and protection of God's Servants is also
of inestimable value for man's proper human and spiritual development. For man today, in his ignorance, ar-
rogance, and metaphysical thirst, is constantly creating
new speculations, metaphysical cults, and methods of self-
realization which neglect or assign secondary importance
to the fundamental teachings of all world religions
(which are the legitimate channels for the slow but safe
improvement and spiritualization of mankind). Few of
the blind leaders of the blind have even bothered to read,
to comprehend, and to live the teachings of the world
religions. The 7 Sacraments, correlated with the 7 lower
Sephiroth, and the 7 Initiations, lead man gradually and
by degrees from animality to spirituality, to true Adepthood--
without getting one lost and confused in the jungles of
homespun speculation and philosophizing.

True Christianity, both exoteric and esoteric, finds its
fulfillment in the Ten Commandments amplified and completed by the Two Commandments of Christ (Love the Lord
thy God with all thy heart, all thy soul, and all thy mind,
and thy fellow-men as thyself." This forms the true basis
of training for genuine Illumination and Adepthood.

You must keep in mind, however, that only preliminary
training is given on the physical plane; the real and advanced training is given on the Inner Planes. True spiritual consciousness transcends both the 5 senses and
psychism. A balanced and healthy character and life must
be achieved before real training can begin.

Our civilization and all of our penal codes ultimately
stand upon the Ten Commandments--which are so much
neglected in the current 'psychic' and 'occult' literature and which are generally despised by modern man.
Only when man has learned to live by the Ten Command-
ments--something which is known to the Higher Powers--
can man begin his real spiritual training.

Man's spiritual consciousness and development depend
upon the activation of his 10 Spiritual Centers or Organs
which are perfectly matched with the Ten Commandments.
The activation of these 'Organs' depend strictly upon
their being used and awakened by appropriate exercises
and by life itself. The Ten Commandments in their
practical applications are very effective and time-
proven set of exercises specifically designed to awaken
our spiritual Centers. As the 22nd chapter of Revelation
puts it: 'Blessed are they that do His Commandments,
that they may have the right to the Tree of Life, and
may enter through the Gates of the City.' And 'to him
that overcometh (the lower self), I shall give the
heavenly Manna (Divine Light), and he will become a
Pillar in my Temple and shall go out (incarnate on earth)
no more.'

The Ten Commandments, being among other things practical
exercises to awaken and activate the 10 spiritual Centers,
must be placed on the Tree of Life and vibrated (i.e.
affirmed) each in its appropriate sphere; then they must
be meditated upon to discover their deeper meanings and
correspondences, and finally, they must be lived and in-
corporated in our being.

Each one of the spiritual Centers is a 'living entity,'
an 'executive' in its respective department. The first
Commandment rules all the others. It is the Divine Spark
in man addressing his human self and the human personality. It affirms its rulership and projects Light into
all the other Centers. Each of these Centers, symbolized
by the sign of a Planet, thus becomes activated in the
constellation. . . which is man! Thus it is that we have
10 Centers to awaken and activate by the Ten Commandments,
to transmute our vices into virtues, our imperfections
and imbalances into perfection and harmony.

Keep in mind the admonition: 'If thou wilt enter into
the consciousness of Life Eternal, keep the Commandments,
practice them, live them, realize them in thyself, become
them.'

Now stand up erect and relaxed, face East and begin with
the affirmation: 'Be silent and know that I am the Lord
thy God' or 'Know ye not that ye are the Temple of the

living God and that the Spirit of God dwells in you.'
(After having gone through the preliminary preparation
of breathing, cleansing, and spiritual awakening
through the Cross Ritual.)."14

What are the central meanings, correspondences, and
practical applications of the Ten Commandments such as I
understand them and as they have been revealed to me at this
point in my spiritual evolution?

A. The Ten Commandments are a set of synthetic formulae
    containing the <u>symbolic</u> representation of the Divine
    Laws and Principles which order and govern all creation,
    from the Spirit (God) to Nature (the physical universe),
    and culminating in Man (humanity).

B. The Ten Commandments have ever expanding meanings, cor-
    respondences, and applications that unfold with the
    heightening and deepening of our consciousness and
    maturity, both within ourselves (at the subjective level)
    and in the world (at the objective level).

C. The Ten Commandments can be looked upon as containing two
    fundamental elements: firstly, the letter, or symbol,
    which is human, culture-bound, relative to the time and
    place which produced them. The letter, or symbol, of
    course, is a finite and closed entity. It is the Spirit,
    or consciousness, which animates and interprets the letter,
    which is universal, infinite, and an open stream of life.
    The key point, therefore, is to connect the letter, or
    symbol, of the Ten Commandments, with their spirit through
    an expanding and maturing consciousness.

D. The Ten Commandments also contain a "science" and an "art,"
    a theoretical framework and a set of guidelines to be ap-
    plied to one's being and daily life, and a set of practical
    exercises designed to activate, cleanse, and coordinate
    the various psychospiritual Centers on the Tree of Life.

E. In conclusion, the Ten Commandments, seen from the eso-
    teric or spiritual viewpoint, are the laws or principles
    that govern the psychospiritual Centers, or Roses, on
    the Tree of Life. They constitute the essence and foun-
    dation of all religions and ethical systems; they order
    and equilibrate all worlds, planes of consciousness, and
    energies, determining their activities and interrelations
    from Spirit to Matter. Thus they are the practical "a,b,c"
    of spiritual life and will accompany the disciple step by
    step on the Path from his very entrance on it to its very
    end, when he will have harmonized and integrated his whole
    nature with their spirit. Then, they will be enscribed
    in "letters of fire" in his own heart and they will be
    an organic part of his being and life. . . and his "pass-
    port" to spiritual Life or Life Eternal.

Having gone through the necessary preamble, let us now look at the Ten Commandments, taken one by one, in terms of their esoteric or spiritual interpretation. The following, of course, is offered by way of example of what can be done with them and is not the only set of esoteric meanings, correspondences, and applications that can be given to them; for these are many, ever changing and deepening with the expansion of human consciousness. They do represent, however, some of the most basic and fundamental ones that can be used both theoretically, for knowledge-getting, and practically, for spiritual growth.

1. <u>I am the Lord thy God, thou shall have no other gods before me</u>.

   "I am" here refers to man's Divine Spark or spiritual Self. "Thou shall have no other gods before me" implies that no other principle or entity in man's being, other than the "Divine Spark," the "small voice within," should become his Center, the integrating and unifying principle of his psyche and life. In man's being and life, there are presently many principles and entities which, in fact, do become, temporarily at least, his "God" or synthesizing Center. These "gods" or partial synthesizing foci can be: his body and its instincts and sensations, his emotions and strong passions, his mind and powerful thoughts or "idée fixes," or even his mystical experiences; the major social roles he plays in society and with which he generally identifies; and, finally, the living or historical "model" of another human being.

   By vibrating and affirming this Commandment in Kether, one temporarily identifies with the spiritual Self, the Divine Spark within, and affirms Its rulership in his being and life, in all of their dimensions and aspects. It affirms, in other words, "let the Divine Spark in me be my true self and rule my being."

   This Commandment thus sums up the whole program of spiritual development; it shows man what he must accomplish while here on earth and helps him to do so temporarily and thus to slowly and gradually bring about this condition on a permanent basis, union with the spiritual Self and Its rulership in our "little kingdom" and in our daily life.

2. <u>Thou shall not make idols of me nor bow down to worship and serve them</u>.

   The key symbol of this Commandment is the word "idols" which comes from the Greek "eidolon," meaning images or thought-forms. This Commandment thus organically continues the process set in motion by the first. It is not enough to affirm that it is the spiritual Self rather than the many "human selves" of man that he should identify with and establish as the Center or unifying principle of his being and life. There is a basic difference between the spiritual Self, Its Life and Consciousness, and the many possible mental representations and symbols that man can create about the spiritual Self during his long evolutionary journey.

This Commandment thus stresses the basic difference between "form" and "force," between a mental representation and a living reality, between a concept and an experience. Consciousness, in order to formulate and to express itself, necessarily needs the twin polarities of form and force, and man must, of necessity, use symbols and representations of Higher Beings, Realities, and states of consciousness, but he can be aware of what they are, a means to an end, and not the end in itself, and thus not confuse them with the reality for which they stand. For man, the ultimate form or vehicle (called "temple" by the various religious traditions) is the psyche, the human aura and the Tree of Life, and not a mental representation.

Man has created countless "idols" or "images" of the spiritual Self which he has represented on icons, statues, or words, and he has worshipped many gods (money, sex, and power being amongst the more popular ones).

This Commandment is designed to help man differentiate between the Divine Spark Itself and Its Life and Consciousness, that reside in the upper reaches of human consciousness, and the many mental representations of It, which are lifeless, that man has and will make of It. This is the affirmation which enables man to distinguish between Creator and Creation, between force and form, and to unite and integrate the two within his consciousness. Vibrated in Chockmah, this affirmation enables man to acquire a true perspective of himself, of his fellow-men, and of God, which is true Wisdom.

3. Thou shall not use the Name of the Lord thy God in vain.

To "use the Name of God in vain" means, exoterically, to use lightly or irreverently any Name of God or Name of Power. Esoterically, however, it means vastly more. The "Name of God" here implies His Presence, His Consciousness, His Life and Energies. This affirmation, therefore, vibrated in Binah, means not to abuse one's being, which is the "temple" of the Divine Spark, in any way--not to misuse or drain one's energies, the Light and Life one receives from "on high," or one's consciousness, emotions, thoughts, and desires in such a way as to cut them off from their central Source, the One Reality or spiritual Self.

Man presently abuses himself and his energies in countless ways on the physical, emotional and mental levels. By not "using the Name of God in vain," man achieves and maintains harmony with his Divine Spark and becomes harmless to other beings. . . and to himself.

4. <u>Thou shall keep holy the day of the Lord thy God</u>.

The key symbols of this Commandment are three: to keep holy, the day of the Lord, and the Lord thy God. "To keep holy" means to preserve the harmony, the relationship or connectedness that will keep something whole or balanced. The "day of the Lord" has several meanings and correspondences, chief of which are: the amount of time dedicated to God, or to direct spiritual work (i.e. establishing contact with the Divine within on the vertical axis through Prayer). It also implies the spiritual plane and spiritual consciousness through which the Divine can be contacted, and the sevenfold cycle of activity in which each phase has its own distinctive characteristics. The "Lord thy God" clearly refers to the Divine Spark at the core of one's being.

One of the most important tasks that man can accomplish while here on earth is to create, to forge and fashion, his own "little world"--to bring about a psychosocial cosmos out of chaos. The creation of man's own universe, furthermore, involves structuring his space, time, and actions. This Commandment, therefore, deals with the proper structuring of man's time so as to make it <u>flow whole</u>, and, therefore, to live a wholesome life.

The major periods of time for man are: the day, the week, the month, and the year. This Commandment calls man's attention to the fact that during each period of time, a day, a week, a month, a year, and even a lifetime, he should periodically set some time aside for turning his focused attention to the Divine within, to actively seek to align his consciousness and life with the Will of the Divine Spark and to raise his consciousness on the Holy Mountain to the point where he can come in conscious contact with the Living Light and Fire, Love and Consciousness of the Divine within.

This means keeping a proper balance and rhythm between Work, Prayer, and Relaxation, between his physical, human, and spiritual activities, and between his professional, personal, and spiritual life, and to tune into the various parts of his being and of the world which are material, psychic, and spiritual in nature.

This affirmation, in short, deals with the mystery of life and growth, of rhythm and of the proper structuring of time, and it focuses man's attention and energies upon Chesed

which is the highest of the psychospiritual Centers which
man can activate while being incarnate on earth, and which
represents Chronos or Time, called by the Greeks the "Father
of the Gods."

5. Thou shall honor thy Father and thy Mother.

The key symbols here are: thou, honor, Father, and
Mother. "Thou" refers to the human self, the conscious,
rational ego acting within the field of consciousness.

"Honor" means: a. To become aware of, to focus one's attention
upon.
b. To enter into a proper relationship with.
c. To give and to receive what is "due."

"Father" means: a. The Spirit which is both within man and
in the world: God and the Divine Spark
which are one in essence.
b. The male principle, the active, dynamic
principle which operates both in man's
being and in his life, in what he is and
in what he does.

"Mother" means: a. Nature, the physical plane which is both
in man (his body) and in the world (the
physical world).
b. The female principle, the passive, receptive principle which operates both in
man's being and in his life, in what he
is and in what he does.

"To honor one's Father and one's Mother" thus means:

a. To become aware that one is both Spirit and Matter and that
so is the world. To enter into a proper relationship
with the Divine Spark and the body within and with God
and Nature in the world. To give and to receive, to abide
by the laws of the Spirit and of Nature--to give God what
is His due and the world what is its due, i.e. to realize
that one has both spiritual and physical needs.

b. To become aware that one is both male and female, and that
there are times when one should act in a dynamic way, affirming one's self and one's ideas, and times when one
should act in a passive way, receiving and accepting what
comes to one.

c. It means to become aware of and to synthesize properly
the myriad of masculine and feminine forces, energies,
and polarieties which constitute and mould our being,
existence, and becoming: the subjective-objective, prayer-
work, knowledge-love, severity-mercy, grace-effort,

asceticism-joie de vivre, joy-pain, spirit-matter, good-evil, accepting one's fate and struggling against it.

This Commandment focuses upon Geburah and awakens it by connecting it with Chesed, synthesizing their energies and principles. It is the Commandment dealing with the mystery of polarity and the realization of synthesis on many levels.

6. Thou shall not kill.

This Commandment implies not to destroy that which exists before its "natural time" for disintegration has come, be it a human being, a creature, an intuition, thought, feeling, aspiration, belief, word, or deed. It is the principle which deals with reverence for life both generically and specifically. It means, essentially, not to create disharmonies, not to interfere with what exists, both within and without one's self, by the imposition of one's will and ideas, but to fulfill one's role, mission, and place in life according to God's Will and thus to consciously harmonize one's self with the Divine Spark and Its Plan of Evolution. This Commandment also deals with unfolding the feminine, receptive, harmonizing principle within one's self and in one's life. It is linked with Tiphareth and activates its energies and principles, synthesizing within itself all that descends from above and all that which ascends from below. For example, to suffocate someone with affection is just as much a violation of this Commandment as it would be starving someone's emotional needs with too much auterity. It is at this level that the true synthesis of Chesed and Geburah, mercy and severity, spirit and matter, male and female is truly realized within one's being and life.

7. Thou shall not commit adultery.

The key symbol here is adultery. From the esoteric standpoint, adultery means to lose the state of pureness and clearness, concentration and integration, that one can possess. It also implies to split or dissociate the psyche from some of its functions, components, and energies. This can take place by desiring, wanting, or willing the wrong thing or the right thing at the wrong time. It means that one should not unite, mate, or establish a circuit (take into one's aura or link one's aura) with the being, energy, or entity which is not for you, which is not on your path of evolution. Properly understood and lived by, it leads one to unite and mate, on all levels, only according to God's Will as this is made manifest in one's being and life. For example, to do something only because it is "practical," "expedient," or easier are all instances of "commiting adultery."

This Commandment focuses on Yesod, activates it, cleanses it, and brings it in proper alignment with the higher Centers and with Malkuth.

10. <u>Thou shall not covet the wife or any of the possessions of thy neighbor</u>.

This is the only Commandment which applies fully and literally to the material plane, as it deals with Malkuth, activating, cleansing, and equilibrating it. It also complements the 7th Commandment on the physical plane as the latter deals with the psychological plane and the motivational dimension.

In essence, it means: you will not desire to receive, be, or become anything but what you are, have, and can become according to the Will and Plan of the Divine Spark. It means that if you see something someone else has that you will not desire to have it, or to be it, without working for it and creating it by your own efforts, once you have obtained the confirmation from the "voice within" that you are doing the right thing. If you violate this Commandment what you would get would not be "yours," organic to your being, but external to you, and a burden for your human and spiritual unfoldment. Also it would most likely generate social conflict and bring about a struggle with others who want to "preserve what they have."

Finally, it also means not to want to evolve too quickly or too slowly, but to wait for the right moment and the natural unfolding of your faculties, energies, joys, and experiences. To give, desire, or accept "gifts" indiscriminately is violating this Commandment. The "wife of thy neighbor" is not only his woman, but also his faculties and his female principle. The "possessions of thy neighbor" are not only what he has and owns but also what he is and has achieved.

All of these Commandments, laws and principles, prepare man, by degrees, to achieve the "incarnation of the Word" or the proper alignment of his human self, from within the center of the field of consciousness, with his spiritual Self, in the superconscious, and to receive an inflow of Life and Light that can permeate his whole being and touch every Center and Plane. Thus the whole Tree is touched and affected, and every principle in man is nourished and aligned with the Divine Spark. Man can mature and grow only through action, through the use of all his faculties and energies; the Ten Commandments are the laws and principles which govern the "right" or harmonious use of all of man's faculties and energies and which make right human relations possible. The "Great Chain of Being" and the inner link and harmony are thus preserved from the Divine to the physical plane.

These Commandments, moreover, have an inner threefold subdivision:

a. The first deals with the Spirit or spiritual Self and Its conscious realization.

b. The second, third, and fourth deal with the manifestation of the Spiritual Light, Fire, and Life in Creation; with preserving the proper alignment, harmony, and flow between the Divine Spark and the various planes of creation, both within and without man.

c. The fifth to the tenth deal, essentially, with the sphere of right human relationships and with the preservation of the proper harmony in one's interpersonal relationships so that the Light and the Life of the Divine Spark can flow through one's Tree of Life and being to others and from others to oneself in an unbroken and undistorted fashion.

If we now take the framework of psychosynthesis and translate the Ten Commandments in terms of its optic and concepts, we readily can see that they contain all the key theoretical steps and practical exercises necessary to achieve a complete psychosynthesis and to consciously complete the creation of one's personality and being.

Thus, the first Commandment points to spiritual psychosynthesis and to Self-identification; making the spiritual Self and true Center and unifying principle of one's psyche and life. The second, third, and fourth point to personal psychosynthesis and to the principle of disidentification and proper energy handling. The fifth to the tenth point to interpersonal psychosynthesis and to the principle of right human relations. Specifically:

1. I am the Lord thy God, thou shall have no other gods before me.

This affirmation clearly deals with Self-identification, with asserting that the Divine Spark is the true Self and not the human self, the psyche, its functions, or any of the social roles that one plays in society.

2. Thou shall not make idols of me.

This affirmation points to the principle of disidentification, warning against the pitfall of making any of the elements of the psyche or of the world the unifying Center of one's being and life.

3. Thou shall not use the name of the Lord thy God in vain.

This injunction deals with the proper use and transformations of spiritual and psychological energies, or with the principle of Alchemy, as it used to be called, or the principle of psychodynamics as it is now called by modern social science.

4. Thou shall keep holy the day of the Lord thy God.

This injunction deals with the principle of timing, rhythm, and cycles. Its aim is to sensitize one to the proper timing and balance in one's growth and daily activities.

5. Thou shall honor thy father and thy mother.

This formula deals with the principle of polarity and gender, of relating properly spirit and matter, male and female, active and passive which is so important in human life.

6. Thou shall not kill.

This injunction deals with the principle of harmony, harmlessness, and proper alignment which is the goal of all true human and spiritual development.

7. Thou shall not commit adultery.

This Commandment deals with the principle of purity and concentration which is vital to achieve anything worthwhile in this world.

8. Thou shall not steal.

This Commandment deals with the principle of honesty and of respect for others.

9. Thou shall not bear false witness.

This injunction deals with the principle of honesty and of objectivity.

10. Thou shall not covet the wife or any of the possessions of thy neighbor.

This injunction deals with the principle of right human relationships and with the principle of personal integrity which are necessary to live in harmony with others in social groups.

Each of the Commandments, or principles, contains a positive and a negative aspect, an aspect of light and an

aspect of darkness, which activate, purify or sully, as-
sociates or dissociates the Centers on the Tree, the Planes
of being, and the spiritual Self with the rest of the personality and with other human beings.

IV. The two royal Commandments of the New Testament.

If the Ten Commandments were the cornerstone of the
Old Testament, the two Commandments given by Jesus are the
cornerstone of the New Testament and, in fact, the synthesis
of all the Commandments--the very foundation of any type of
genuine spiritual work. These two Commandments are: "Thou
shall love the Lord thy God with all thy heart, all thy soul,
and all thy mind, and thy fellow-men as thyself."

Though countless explanations, on different levels of
consciousness and being, could be given of these two Commandments, we shall limit ourselves to the most basic implications and applications.

These two Commandments depict symbolically the interrelationship between the Trinity (Father, Son, and Holy Spirit;
Wisdom, Love, and Will; God, Man, and Nature; the spiritual,
the psychic, and the physical Planes) and Duality (God and
Man, Spirit and Matter, Male and Female). As such, they show
man how he can consciously cooperate in his becoming, in the
fashioning and forging of his being, and in the realization
of his perfection. Thus, they deal with the mysteries of the
Trinity and of Duality with their ever-expanding meanings,
correspondences, and applications on the different planes of
consciousness and being.

Man, who is an objectified and manifested emanation of
the Trinity (i.e. who is a triune being: spiritual, psychic,
and physical; the being in whom force and form express as
consciousness; the being whose key attributes and needs are
Wisdom, Love, and Life) and who is the microcosm of the macrocosm, has his being and operates both in the outer, or objective, world (the horizontal axis) and in the inner, or
subjective, world (the vertical axis) and in the inner, or
subjective, world (the vertical axis) and is thus a dual being.
He must grow and expand both inwardly and outwardly. What
flows into him from the higher reaches of his psyche must
manifest itself outwardly, in the world. This is the philosophical key to both genuine human development and to true
spiritual life, as it is the foundation of the Great Work.
It is also the cognitive handle by which to make Faith and any
ritual come alive and become effective.

Let us first look at this injunction in terms of the mysteries of Duality, which it symbolizes, and then in terms of the mysteries of the Trinity which are also contained symbolically therein. Love, Mystics have unanimously claimed, is both the first and the greatest creative force in the universe, as it is the manifestation of God's Will. The two most basic expressions of love, which embody the deepest needs and drives of man, are the love of God and the love of man (the third being the love of nature which is God in manifestation). Unless man learns, consciously and concretely, how to love both God and man, he will never achieve any truly great thing as he will be cut off from the very roots of life. And it can safely be said that one of the greatest dilemmas of man is that of reconciling and integrating properly the love of God, spiritual love, and the love of man, human and physical love.

The whole life and growth of man really revolves around the double movement of introflection and extroflection, of interiorization and exteriorization, of drawing the Light and Fire from the heights of his being to express them, in a concrete and constructive fashion, through his words and actions, in the world. The progressive expansion of human consciousness, which is the Great Work of man, involves drawing ever higher "psychic voltage," or "life," to which he must give definite sociocultural forms and expressions in the world.

The whole of spiritual life, moreover, revolves around the twin concepts of worship (which represents the expression of the love of God) and of service (which represents the expression of the love of man). Putting these together, we have the Cross of the vertical axis thrusting towards God and the horizontal axis thrusting towards man which, graphically, forms the cornerstone of the true spiritual life and of the Great Work.

In order to be able to give, man must have, and to have he must receive, thus establishing a self-sustaining cycle between these two polarities. Through worship, expressed mainly through Prayer, man must travel inwards and upwards towards the levels of the superconscious wherein dwells the Divine Spark. He must slowly and gradually climb the sacred Mountain at the top of which the spiritual Self will manifest Itself and bestow upon the human self Light and Fire: knowledge, love, and life. Then, through service, expressed mainly through work and altruistic love, man must use and share with others what he has received from the Divine Spark. . . for unless he does so, the Light and Fire will cease to flow and to manifest themselves.

Introverts generally turn first towards the Spirit within and then towards their fellow-men, learning how to love men through their love for God, while extroverts generally turn

first towards their fellow-men, learning to love God through
their love for man. Without renewing oneself on the holy
Mountain through the spiritual Light and Fire, man would grow
tired and stale, and would not have anything truly valuable
to offer his fellow-men. Without using and sharing what
he has received from his Divine Spark with his fellow-men,
the disciple would soon lose his inspiration and cease to
receive more from within. Hence, both polarities are equally
important and complement each other. Prayer cannot truly
function without work nor work without prayer.

Turning to the framework of psychosynthesis, we find
the same principle of Duality expressed in different terms.
The two fundamental aims of psychosynthesis are first self-
actualization and then (or better yet: concomitantly) Self-
realization. The love of God must be balanced by the love
of man, interiorization by exteriorization, worship by service,
and prayer by work.

When it comes to the mysteries of the Trinity, these
are many and are, ultimately, unfathomable as they expand
and widen with the growth of human consciousness and new
levels of emergence. One of the most basic and practical
applications of these mysteries, which is explicitly alluded
to by this injunction, is that dealing with Faith and with
the effective worship of God.

Faith, spiritually speaking, is both a spiritual gift
and the fruit of human labor; it is the focused convergence of
concentration, love, and will upon one central point.   Thus,
the three royal faculties of the human psyche: knowing, loving,
and willing must bring their gifts, human knowledge, human love,
and human creative energy, that these may be amplified and
spiritualized by the Divine Light and Fire of the spiritual
Self. Effective worship, therefore entails focusing all of
one's love ("all thy heart"), all of one's attention or concentration ("all thy soul"), and all of one's knowledge ("all
thy mind") upon each word, symbol, or gesture of the Ritual
which is offered to the spiritual Self as a "vehicle of expression," to bring life to the Ritual and to connect it with
the "spirit behind the letter."

Love and concentration are faculties which one acquires
through life's experiences by using them. Knowledge, in this
case, is acquired by repeated meditation (male polarity) and
by contemplation (female polarity) on the given symbol and
ritual.

To truly love the Divine, both within oneself and in
the world, and to love one's fellow-men as oneself is to live
the spiritual life, this is what we have come on earth to learn
and to do gradually and on ever-expanding levels of consciousness and being. To truly love God means, ultimately, to become

one with Him and to truly love our fellow-men, likewise, means to become properly related to them. Thus this injunction leads, by degree, to the return of the Many to the One. This interiorization (climbing the holy Mountain to receive Grace: Light, Fire, and Life) and exteriorization (working and sharing with others), prayer and work, receiving and giving, generates a self-starting and self-perpetuating cycle, the one activating the other and dynamizing both in the process. This is the "living" of the greatest of all Commandments or, at least, as much as can be said about it in human words!

CHAPTER XII

CONCLUSION: THE NATURE AND USE OF RITUAL

Next to the introduction and the present conclusion, the core of this boook is made up of 12 basic lectures which I have given, at first separately as autonomous units and then as an integrated seminar over a period of about 7 years. Many topics and subjects have been touched upon, basically from the perspective of the Spiritual Tradition, dealing with the nature and purpose of man, with the meaning of the universe and of life, with the nature of and man's relationship to God, with the Great Work, spirituality and the unfoldment of spiritual consciousness, and, particularly, with the nature and use of Ritual as this is applied to the great "Seven Fundamentals" of the Christian tradition.

This work formed the central core of my deepest interests and aspirations for a period of about 20 years. During that time, many hours were spent reading, meditating, praying, travelling, and discussing these questions with other people who were both more and less qualified than myself. What I was after was, on the one hand, to provide satisfying answers to the deepest questions that were ever formulated within my consciousness and to find a practical and effective "art of living" that would enable me to develop the highest and best in myself, so that I could make my greatest contributions to others, and, in the process, live the most constructive, creative, and fulfilling life. On the other hand, I was also after a simple and practical system that would offer direct, practical, and satisfying answers to what I feel are the fundamental questions and quests of our age, at least for some "kindred souls."

To get to the point where I am now, and to formulate the key lectures of this book, I experimented widely with many different approaches, ranging from the psychological to the spiritual via various so called "esoteric" and "occult" systems. I studied the teachings of different religions, esoteric schools and orders, and explored the various approaches of humanistic and transpersonal psychology. By and large, I found that every religion, school or approach did offer something, that it did contain one or two rays of that "ineffable Light and Truth" I was seeking, but that none could offer the whole or, rather, the "ready-made system" I could apply to my own unique being and life. Thus, after much reflection and experimentation, I gleaned the best I could find from these many different traditions and came up with the approach that is outlined in this book. In formulating this approach, I was guided by three major criteria:

a. The esoteric language, the great complexities and intracacies of different systems must be made simple and readily comprehensible to a sincere and mature person.

b. This approach must be practical, that is, it must be capable of being lived and incarnated in one's life and being in the existing sociocultural conditions of the modern world and in the unique situation of each interested person, and it must yield tangible and constructive fruits or changes.

c. It must go to the "essence of things," touch and incorporate what is most important or go to the "heart of the spiritual quest."

d. Last but not least, it must be safe and lead one to greater psychological health and integration, and to a more productive and satisfying everyday life; it must enable one to have a fuller and richer social, personal, and professional life, and not make one a recluse, an eccentric character, or a person engrossed in his own self and particular interests and exercises.

While neither religion nor the best of the human sciences, nor even the various esoteric schools and orders I came in contact with provided a ready-made answer and system; a combination and synthesis of all of these produced the approach I am offering in this book. This approach is far from being a "system" or another "school," for it is not finished and requires much work, development, and further refinements and additions. Yet, I do believe that it can provide a sincere and mature seeker with some of the essential keys, sources, and exercises to "launch him on his way" and to enable him to find his own distinctive development and synthesis. All I can vouch for is that it has proven highly creative and rewarding in my own life and in the lives of many students who have worked and experimented with the principles and guidelines provided by this approach, and I am still working with it, ever refining it, and discovering new meanings, correspondences, and applications for it.

The central points that were discussed in this work are:

1. That we are now living in an age in which a major intellectual and cultural revolution is taking place, leading to an integral vision of reality that is grounded in a trinitarian view of knowledge, man, and the world as being physical, psychic, and spiritual.

2. That the truly fundamental problems and questions of our age, as perhaps those of any age in human history, cannot be satisfactorily answered from the perspective of either sensory, affective, or intellectual conscious-ness (i.e. that science, philosophy, and religion, in their present state, cannot, by their very level of ap-proach and interpretation, provide these answers) but only from the perspective of a higher and qualitatively different state of consciousness which has traditionally been called "spiritual consciousness."

3. That this being so, the systematic transformation, ex-pansion, deepening and heightening of human consciousness, leading to spiritual consciousness, is now the foremost prerequisite for man and humanity to take their next step in evolution.

4. That this transformation--expansion, deepening, and heightening--of human consciousness must be a conscious endeavor which involves all the functions of the psyche as well as higher energies and inspiration than those which can be provided by the personality of a human being as it is now structured.

5. That the knowledge, the effective means, and the proper motivation necessary to bring about the dawning of spir-itual consciousness can best be distilled from a creative amalgamation and synthesis of the best of the modern human sciences with the best of the sacred traditions.

6. That this new and qualitatively different state of con-sciousness is the product of both a new way of life, traditionally called "living the Life" and of "Prayer" as interpreted in its technical sense.

7. That Prayer, as defined by the sacred traditions, implies both a female and a male aspect; the first being known as "Entering the Silence" or consciously heightening one's sensitivity and receptivity, while the second being known as "Ritual" or consciously heightening the flow of psychic energies (the Light, Fire, and Life of the spiritual Self) flowing through our field of consciousness.

8. That the development of spiritual consciousness involves the double quest for God and for His Church, the discovery of the spiritual Self and the development and coordination of the personality system to enable the attributes of the former to manifest in the world through the latter, and which modern humanistic psychology calls self-actualization and Self-realization.

9. That the knowledge and training of the will provided by the Occult and Magical Traditions must be balanced and directed by the unfoldment of love and faith provided by the religious and mystical approaches.

10. That the ultimate core and substance of consciousness-expansion and spiritual development is the love of God and the love of man--the love of life. All other approaches are but indirect means to that end.

11. That true spiritual work and the dawning of spiritual consciousness, or the breakthrough of the superconscious into conscious, involves both a male, or psychological part, which depends on the student, and a female, or spiritual part, which is a free gift of the spiritual Self and which lies outside the province of the will of the student.

12. That the Great Work is, ultimately, what all human beings have come to achieve on earth, and what they are consciously or unconsciously pursuing.

Within this general framework, we have seen that all religions have three fundamental parts: a body, a soul, and a spirit; and that it is the "soul" of religion which is presently "sick," and which must be furnished with a new explanation and interpretation which is congruent with the needs, ideals, and experiences of people living in today's world. We have also seen that all religions come from the same source and have the same basic goal: to lead human beings to a conscious union with the Divine. As there is one God, one basic Reality, and one common trunk for all external religions, their basic essentials are the same. In the Western Spiritual Tradition, we have identified this central core with the "Seven Fundamentals" which have their functional equivalents in all other great religions and which, when properly understood and applied, will lead any human being to his spiritual Initiation or Illumination.

We have looked at these Seven Fundamentals as including all the knowledge, the training, and the key exercises which are needed to have an integrated and effective curriculum in spiritual development. These Fundamentals were then shown to provide a training ground for all the key functions of the psyche and their major processes, namely for training:

a. The will through concentration and affirmation.
b. Thinking through meditation.
c. Feeling through adoration and devotion.
d. Imagination through visualization and, later, visions.
e. Intuition through aspiration and inspiration, invocation and evocation.
f. Sensations through observation and sensory awareness.
g. Biopsychic drives and impulses through self-mastery and transmutation.

These Fundamentals were also shown as providing an ideal training ground for concentration, meditation, contemplation, and theurgy or invocation-evocation. To be sure, these basic aspects of the spiritual life can also be developed with other materials, images, and blue-prints but, those provided by the Seven Fundamentals are both very rich and fruitful, safe and time-proven, and integrated within the religious life of most people (with their functional equivalents in other religions) and thus they furnish an excellent starting point. The practical outline that was suggested was to take each of the Fundamentals, to identify its key symbols, petitions, and affirmations, and to use these singly, as a group, or as a whole to:

a. Develop concentration.
b. Practice meditation and decipher their inner meanings, associations, correspondences, and applications.
c. Practice contemplation and get at their very heart and substance.
d. Practice theurgy and fill one's field of consciousness with higher Energies and Inspiration.
e. Construct practical thought-forms to then slowly develop, concretize, and incarnate them in one's being and life.

The standard procedure here would be for someone who has become dissatisfied with what he is and with his present life, and who is aspiring to become more than what he is-- to transcend himself and to have a life more abundant--to take one of the Fundamentals and to work with it for a certain period of time, ranging from a minimum of one week to a maximum of one year for each one; to carefully train his psychological functions with it, to slowly decipher and expand its meanings, associations, correspondences, and applications, and to use it theurgically as a whole to awaken the intuitive flow and a higher state of consciousness. Then, he should carefully record in a journal, or workbook, the results that have been obtained. The same can then be done with all the other Fundamentals, or with any basic document of any sacred tradition. Each year, the same procedure can be repeated so that all Fundamentals are gone through again and that one can note how much progress has, indeed, been made during the year, and how much one's consciousness and intuitive grasp have, in fact, developed.

The Fundamentals can be used, in their various work phases, either alone or with a group of like-minded and interested people, and in one's Church during the regular Sunday services or shortly thereafter. Their treasures and depth are practically inexhaustible and ever-expanding with the growth of one's consciousness. The subjects they deal with and the powers and forces they work with are not only time-proven and greatly energized in the psychic atmosphere

of a Western nation, but they are also safe from the many
subjects and areas that could be dangerous for the sanity,
mental balance, and personality integration of an average
person who becomes interested in self-development and in
the spiritual life.

Before true spiritual training and work can be started,
a minimum of self-knowledge, self-mastery, and self-
integration are a sine qua non. Here, I cannot recommend
too strongly that interested students undergo some form of
humanistic therapy (Jungian, Gestalt, or Psychosynthesis)
to achieve this preliminary phase. The traditions of well-
established and authentic Esoteric Orders or the guidance
of a wise and loving person are also invaluable and to be
greatly recommended. While it is possible for some people
to do this work alone and to achieve the great prize of spiritual Illumination, it is much safer and more practical for
most people to follow the other route with objective checks
and the guidance of other, more advanced people.

I would be very interested in hearing from individuals
or groups who plan to work on a serious basis with the Fundamentals as I have outlined them. Thus, I invite them to
contact me through my publisher so that we can have some feed-
back: that I may learn about the results they are obtaining
by following this method and that I may inform them of further
developments and experiments that I may be involved with at the
time.

This book is but the beginning of a very long and ex-
citing adventure; there will be further books and, hopefully,
some form of contact will be established between interested
readers and seekers, the groups I will organize, and the work
I will be doing. May the Spirit grant that we meet and join
efforts, and may He inspire us all for the accomplishment of
the Great Work.

THE END

FOOTNOTES

1: SRIA Documents

2: _Cloud_, p. 18.

3: Ibid., pp. 15-16-22.

4: SRIA Documents

5: _Invocation._, p. 10.

6: Ibid., p. 32.

7: _Cloud_, p. 44.

8: SRIA Documents, Bishop Theodotus

9: Ibid.

10: _Cloud_, p. 85.

11: SRIA Documents

12: SRIA Documents, Bishop Theodotus

13: Ibid.

14: Ibid.

APPENDIX A

THE HUMAN PSYCHE

Its Nature and Structure: its Functions, their Development and Use

In the turbulent, bewildering, and fascinating era we are now living in which is, indeed, a transitional period in which an old world is dying and a new world is being born, a fundamental consensus is slowly emerging amongst students of the human and social sciences as well as amongst students of the psychic and spiritual disciplines. This cognitive convergence and crystallizing consensus asserts, briefly, that:

a. Of all knowledge open to a human being, self-knowledge is both the most important and the indispensable prerequisite to acquire any other kind of systematic knowledge.

b. Of all mastery open to a human being, self-mastery is both the most important and the logical starting point lest a veritable box of pandora be open with every new form of energy and control that man acquires.

c. Of all quests open to a human being, the quest for self-actualization and the quest for self-realization are the most important ones which should also precede the other manyfold quests that the human adventure makes available.

At the foundation of self-knowledge, self-mastery, self-actualization and Self-realization and at their very core stands a proper understanding of the human psyche, its nature and structures; its functions and their dynamics, unfoldment, and manifestation. It is a systematic exploration, analysis, and description of these that will constitute the subject matter of the present essay.

Another area of general consensus which is also slowly emerging and crystallizing today amongst concerned and mature thinkers is that the history of man is really the biography of the unfoldment and expression of human consciousness; and that the existential essence of man is his human consciousness and not his biological organism or his Divine Spark. Finally, it is also more and more agreed upon by avant-garde thinkers that it is upon human consciousness and its quantitative and qualitative expansion and transformation that the thrust of the evolutionary forces is focused upon.

One of the most important and perennial questions that human beings have always asked and answered in different ways is: What is human consciousness and its matrix, the human psyche? The term "psyche" is the Greek

126

word which is now generally used by the human and social sciences to designate what used to be called the "soul" of man's human nature. It is the "matrix," the seat or structures, through which human consciousness emerges, flows, and manifests itself. The psyche is thus the "house," the "temple," or the composite vehicle of human consciousness. The sacred traditions generally subdivided it into the <u>animal</u>, <u>human</u>, and <u>spiritual</u> soul, body, or consciousness, which is made up of what the Ancients called the Four Elements (Earth, Water, Air, and Fire) and that modern mystics and spiritual scientists call the <u>etheric</u>, <u>astral</u>, <u>mental</u>, and <u>spiritual</u> "body." As these cannot be seen by the naked eye or through a microscope (though they can be seen by clairvoyant sight and now seen through special screens and even photographed by the Kirlian method), they have not yet been studied by the human and social sciences which have, most of the time, denied their existence.

Since the second half of the 19th century, however, a number of independent and mystically or occultly oriented thinkers such as Helena Blavatsky, Rudolph Steiner, Max Heindel, George Plummer, George Gurdjieff, and others have again become vitally concerned with the question of the existence, the nature, and the manifestations of the human soul and have formulated unusual philosophies and methodologies to integrate the body of their studies and conclusions. A few great academicians such as Henri Bergson, Pitirim Sorokin, and Pierre Theilhard de Chardin have travelled along the same tracks and have come up with, basically, the same assumptions and conclusions. In the last 3 decades several humanistic and transpersonal psychologists have also become fascinated with the question of the human soul and its higher reaches and potentialities. Beginning with William James and Jung and continuing with Maslow and Assagioli, new models of the psyche, its nature, structures, and functions have been proposed. With the "rediscovery" and renewed emphasis upon the will, the superconscious, the inner spaces and latent energies of the psyche, and the transpersonal energies, the following model has finally crystallized, constituting the latest and most sophisticated model of the psyche we have up to now.

The structure of the psyche

Basic model: Advanced model:

Where the basic terms are defined as:

Superconscious: those levels and energies of human consciousness lying
above the threshold of consciousness and deriving their
being from the Spiritual Self. It is the seat and the
source of intuitions, inspirations of a lofty religious,
artistic, philosophic, or scientific nature, the creations
of genius, sainthood, and heroism.

Higher Subconscious: those levels and energies of human consciousness that
stand between and filter the materials between the
Superconscious and the conscious.

Preconscious: those levels of human consciousness that stand on the very
threshold of the conscious but which have not yet penetrated
into its field.

Field of Consciousness: the stream of awareness made up of the "7 functions"
which manifest through speaking and acting and
which derive their energies from the human self.

Lower subconscious: those levels and energies of human consciousness that
stand and filter the materials between the conscious
and the unconscious. Materials which have been forgotten and repressed and which are gathered from the
entire range of human experience.

Unconscious: those levels and energies of human consciousness lying below
the threshold of consciousness which derive their being from
the biopsychic organism of man. The psychic energies that
govern the organic life of the body: the seat of the basic
instincts and drives such as sexuality, self-preservation, and
aggressiveness. Here are also found complexes having strong
emotional charges that are produced by traumas, psychic conflict, and very painful and threatening experiences.

     Simply put, these various areas of the psyche represent the consciousness
of the Spiritual Self (the Superconscious) which have not yet been brought
into the field of consciousness and which theology called the personal "heaven";
the consciousness of the psyche, or human self, (the subconscious, preconscious, and field of consciousness) which are partially within and partially
without the field of consciousness and which theology called "purgatory" and
"earth" respectively; and the consciousness of the biopsychic organism which
lies outside the field of consciousness and which theology called "hell."
Three major branches of contemporary psychology are now dealing specifically
with each of these areas of "consciousness"; these are: psychoanalysis, or
depth psychology, which focuses on the unconscious, existential psychology
which focuses on the conscious, pre-conscious, and subconscious, and finally
"height" or transpersonal psychology which focuses on the superconscious.
The conscious, however, can be systematically expanded into the unconscious
and materials and energies coming from the unconscious, the subconscious,
and the superconscious can find entry into the field of consciousness thus
realizing within man the central injunction of science: from the known to the
unknown.

The functions of the psyche

The psyche

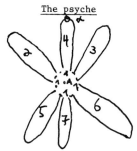

The basic terms are defined as:

♦: The Spiritual Self, the Divine Spark, the ontological essence of man.
A: The human self, the conscious ego directing the 7 functions of the psyche.
1: The will, the focused energies of the human self which activate and propel all the other functions.
2: Thinking, the mental process by which one grasps and makes sense of reality and of one's experiences in the world.
3: Feeling, energies issuing from the human self which impinge upon the field of consciousness and elicit a response. Example: joy, sorrow, surprise, awe, fear, excitement, etc.
4: Intuition, "seeing from within" or the "teaching from within," the spiritual function of the psyche through which a breakthrough of the superconscious takes place into the conscious.
5: Imagination, the image-making function which can reproduce any of the other functions within the field of consciousness and which is synthetic in nature. It has a receptive or female polarity and a creative or male polarity.
6: Biopsychic drives, impulses-desires, the basic drives of the body, such as hunger, thirst, fatigue, and of repressed instincts and painful experiences.
7: Sensations, external stimuli impinging upon the field of consciousness and eliciting a response. Example: seeing, hearing, tasting, smelling, and touching.

The first step, in exploring and analyzing the field of consciousness, is to have a map or a set of categories with which to denote the different energies and materials that flow through the field of consciousness. This "map" is provided by the 7 functions aforementioned. The second step is to be able to identify, at any given moment, the operation of these 7 functions, to recognize them experientially and to distinguish one from the other. The third step is to be able to deliberately train and further develop each function by a series of specific and efficient exercises. The fourth step is to coordinate and integrate these functions around the human self. The fifth and last step consists in having the Spiritual Self express Its energies and consciousness through the human self and through each of these functions.

After one has achieved a good theoretical and experiential grasp
of the field of consciousness, one can continue and extend the exploration and analysis to the realms of the subconscious, the unconscious
and the superconscious.

To do so both productively and safely one should be very familiar
with the 7 functions of the psyche and have acquired a good control and
coordination of them through various appropriate exercises. To provide
an overall sense of timing, keep in mind that some schools dedicate one
year's work for the proper exploration, analysis, development, and coordination of the field of consciousness after which another year is
spent on the exploration and interpretation of the unconscious and another
year yet for the exploration and interpretation of the superconscious.
Thus it is only at the end of the 3 years' work that the truly serious
and systematic work really begins!

While all 7 functions are important and equally part of the psyche
and of the personality, there are 5 of them that are especially important
for the inner work, both at the psychological and at the spiritual level.
These, therefore, must be understood, consciously trained, and coordinated
to begin the true work on the personality and the individuality (the
lower consciousness and the higher consciousness). These are:

1. The will which must be understood in its nature and dynamics and
    experienced in its manifestations, and, naturally, properly trained
    and developed.
2. Thinking which must be understood in its nature and dynamics and
    experienced in its manifestations, and properly developed and trained.
3. Feeling which must be understood in its nature and dynamics and ex-
    perienced in its manifestations, and cultivated and consciously
    directed.
4. Imagination which must be understood in its nature and dynamics, in
    its polarity and consequences, and which must be experienced and
    also properly developed and cultivated.
5. Intuition which must be understood in its nature and dynamics, in
    its polarity and "trigger mechanism," and which must be experienced,
    cultivated, and differentiated from emotion, impulse, and instinct.

The will is harnessed and applied through the process known as
concentration and affirmation; thinking is harnessed and applied through
the process known as meditation with its various stages; feeling is harnessed
and applied through the process known as devotion and adoration; imagination
is harnessed and applied through the process known as visualization and its
various steps and degrees; and finally intuition is "triggered" and turned
on through the process known as invocation and evocation which bring about
a genuine breakthrough of the superconscious into the conscious, which
opens up various "doors" and "layers" of the psyche through which different energies and materials can flow into the field of consciousness.

The inner work of man (work on the personality and on the self
rather than action in the world) is based on the systematic and developmental use of these processes on all of their levels: psychological

131

(development of the personality), <u>psychic</u> (exploration and use of the latent energies of the mind as in parapsychology, psychism, or witch-craft), and <u>spiritual</u> (exploration and alignment with the will and energies of the spiritual Self).   These, therefore, are the true <u>tools</u> or <u>instruments</u> that are used by the practical man, the scientist, and the artist as well as by the magician, the occultist, and the mystic though, naturally, on different levels of operation and amplification. The three highest types of human beings known and venerated by human history, the sage, the saint, and the hero are actually personality types in which <u>thinking</u>, <u>feeling</u>, and <u>will</u> have been purified, organized, exhalted, and properly aligned with the higher energies and will of the spiritual Self.

To begin a genuine and sequential work on one self and one's personality it is thus of paramount importance to understand, to work with, and to train these various functions.   There is no substitute for this work and by-passing it or engaging in it in a haphazard or negligent fashion can be very detrimental and delusional for anyone.

APPENDIX B

THE INTUITION

Its Nature, Components, and Proper Development

In a previous paper, we have outlined the nature, structure, and
functions of the psyche, and we have briefly discussed their tremendous
importance as a foundation for genuine and systematic work on one's self
and personality. In this essay we shall focus upon one of the basic
functions of the psyche, the intuition, and present an in-depth exploration
and analysis of its nature and operation as well as the basic procedure
by which to activate it and work with it.

While all 7 functions have various aspects and dimensions, including
the biopsychic one (unconscious), the psychological one (conscious), and
the spiritual one (superconscious), it is intuition that is the distinc-
tively spiritual function of the psyche and, as such, perhaps the most
misunderstood one and the least developed at this stage in human evolution.
It is intuition which links the superconscious with the conscious and that
connects the spiritual Self with the human self. It is through intuition
that higher energies and materials are brought through into the field of
consciousness and made available to the human self and the other functions.
It is through intuition that the will, the energies, and the higher faculties of the Self and the superconscious are manifested, that new "doors"
are open in the psyche and new layers of consciousness activated. Intuition is thus the "language of the Spirit" and the channel established
between our present center of consciousness and a much higher one of which
we are not conscious as yet.

The specific "language" or "units" of intuition are symbols or
archetypes with their peculiar nature, dynamics, and transpersonal quality.
Just as words and concepts are the language of the conscious mind so symbols
are the language of the Deeper mind, of the superconscious and the unconscious, and their essence are intuitions with their accompanying energies
and not thoughts or feelings. Symbols are also consciousness focusers,
transmittors, and transformers with a multi-layered structure and are dynamic.
To understand and work with intuition it is, therefore, imperative to
understand and to be able to work with symbols.

It is very easy to confuse intuition with impulse, instincts, and
emotions, and most people, in fact, do that, with tragic consequences
which have veiled and degraded the true nature and function of intuition
which is, in fact, quite different and coming from quite another level than
the former. Etymologically speaking, intuition means to "see through" or
"see from within" and it also means the "teaching from within"; to "see"

132

the Spirit and learn from the Spirit rather than from the world, from our body, or from our personality and its human experience. Our eyes, or rather attention, can be focused, externally, upon the world, upon humanity, or upon God, and, internally, it can be focused upon our biopsychic organism, our psychosocial nature, the personality, or upon the Divine Spark. Intuition is focusing our attention or "inner eye" upon the spiritual Self and upon God and establishing an inner dialogue with Him. From this we can see its tremendous importance and the necessity to train it and develop it properly.

Several thinkers, from Bergson to Assagioli through Sorokin, see intuition as the next central faculty that humanity has to develop on its evolutionary path, and some of them go as far as saying that, unless we do develop our latent intuitive powers, we shall not be able to survive the present world-crisis and transitional epoch, let alone take our next individual and collective step in evolution. As far back as the Greeks we have the statement that: man learns first and is con- trolled by physis, nature, then he learns through and is controlled by ethos, society, and finally that he will learn through and be controlled by logos, the Divine within and without. Bergson rearticulated this position when he stated that: for many thousands of years man functioned, like the animals still do, through his instincts which provided him with an instinctive harmony with nature and with his biological organism; then man left nature for society where he functions through his reason and the laws of his society which provide a conscious but tenuous and fluctuating harmony with his personality and his sociocultural environment; finally, man will yet function through a higher principle, intuition, which he defined as "self-conscious instinct," "instinct" coming not from the body and nature but from the spiritual Self and God which will usher humanity into the Kingdom of God. Sorokin saw intuition as the central faculty and fountain-head through which all major discoveries and cultural creations were brought into being—as man's highest faculty. Lastly Assagioli saw intuition as the faculty which we must now consciously develop. . . or perish as an ascending and evolving species. This because, for him, only intuition can now provide the insights and the understanding that we need to understand ourselves and others, to establish right human relationships and acquire the necessary self-knowledge and self-mastery which our scientific and technological achievements (the harnessing and utilization of powerful physical energies) are now making more and more mandatory if we are to respond creatively to our present impass and world-crisis. Finally, he also claimed that it is only through intuition that human beings will realize the principle of essential divinity within themselves and in the world, and which is now necessary for us to continue our psychological and spir- itual development and to meet effectively the problems and dilemmas we are, in one way or another, all confronted with.

Briefly put, intuition implies going from a given premise to its conclusion without going through the intervening mental and logical steps and to grasp the true essence and nature of anything, be it in the world or in man. Even a little reflection will show how it is this ability that human beings now need so desperately as they waddle through great inner and outer confusion, tensions, and conflicts. There is hardly a problem on which intuition cannot shed a most needed light; in fact, there are

inner and outer, individual and collective, problems and dilemmas
that only intuition can solve at this point when our energy sources
are being rapidly depleted and when another world war would wipe out
life on this planet. In fact, the fundamental questions that have
always existed for humanity and that each generation and each culture
have had to provide tentative answers to--the riddle of the Sphinx,
who am I, where do I come from, where am I going, what am I doing here
on earth, and how can I live the most constructive and creative life;
the enigma of the universe, why is there a universe and what is its
purpose? What is man's purpose in the universe?; and the puzzle of life,
what is life, where does it come from, what is its destiny, and how can
I achieve a more conscious and abundant life--can, at the present moment,
be answered satisfactorily only from the standpoint of an active and
creative intuition.

While intuition is not, in its true nature and essence, a psychological faculty but rather a spiritual faculty with a different origin,
structure, and manifestation, it does require the proper use of the 4
major psychological faculties: willing, thinking, feeling, and imagination
and the proper development and use of their major processes: concentration,
meditation, prayer, and visualization.

Their combined and properly coordinated use yields what has been
called aspiration which is used through the process of invocation, and which
constitutes the male polarity of intuition, the human effort or Promethean
thrust pointing upwards. To this male polarity, or conscious elevation
and ascent of the center of consciousness, corresponds a female polarity
of intuition, or inspiration manifesting through the process of evocation,
which is the answer of the spiritual Self to the longings and askings of
the human self, the Divine Grace or Epimethean response, which descends
and reveals itself in the center of consciousness. Diagrammatically represented, we have the following schema:

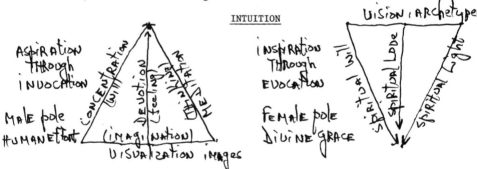

Thus to establish an active and creative intuitive flow or to activate
the energies and manifestations of the intuition, we must focus all of our
trained human will, concentration, upon the spiritual Self, all of our
thinking, meditation, upon the spiritual Self, all of our feeling, prayer,
upon the spiritual Self, and finally all our imagination, visualization,
upon the spiritual Self. The "answer" or revelation will then come in the

form of a vision (transforming our imagination), of spiritual will
(revealing the will of the Divine Spark and energizing our human will to
carry it out), of spiritual love (transforming and exhalting our human
feelings and desires), and of contemplation (revealing to our consciousness
the "Mysteries of the Kingdom," manifesting the spiritual truths and
laws of our being and of the world). To aspiration thus corresponds
inspiration and invocation is followed by evocation and in the process
a channel or bridge is established between the superconscious and the
conscious, between the spiritual Self and the human self through which many
energies, materials and illuminations will flow.

True prayer, in its female aspect of entering the silence or
heightening sensibility and receptivity and in its male aspect of ritual
or heightening the psychic voltage and energies available to the human self
and the functions of the psyche, is designed to do exactly the same thing
even though it uses a different terminology and approach, for the great
truths and principles are the same for all ages, cultures, and human beings.

Unless man does his own distinctive work and part in the whole process,
no answer and revelation will come for the Spiritual Powers do not promote
"spiritual laziness" and do need human, conscious cooperation. Moreover,
the spiritual energies cannot operate in a psychological vacuum, they can
only work with and transform, exhalt, and amplify that which is offered.
Thus, the first part of the Great Work must be the human, psychological
part--the proper training, understanding, and gradual development of the
will, thought, feeling, and imagination through their respective processes
of concentration, meditation, devotion, and visualization. There is simply
no substitute for that work and it is a prerequisite for the spiritual
work that will follow and complete the operation.

A last important question which is generally asked and which must
be answered correctly is: how do I discern what is truly intuition from
what might be impulse, instinct, or emotion? How do I know that what I
am "seeing," "hearing," or "contacting" does in fact come from the spiritual
Self and not from the body, the personality, or the world with its many
agents and subtle influences? While this is far more a question of direct
personal experience rather than of definition or intellectual analysis, the
following can be said as general guidelines:

1. The true voice of intuition always speaks very softly and gently;
    thus one must be sensitive and receptive enough to grasp it and not
    have it drowned out by the sensations, stimuli, noises, and other
    distractions which come from our own being or from the world and
    which generally fill both our minds and hearts. In other words, one
    must have achieved a good enough level of disidentification with the
    body, with the emotions, with the mind, and with the outer world
    before genuine intuition can be received and acknowledged. . . let
    alone properly interpreted.

2. True intuition as the voice of the Divine Spark never coerces anyone
    to do anything whereas impulses, instincts, emotions, and influences
    from the personality and the world pressure and coerce us. As an old

proverb puts it: God never coerces anyone but waits patiently until He is Loved, Desired, and Bid to manifest Himself but the Devil
does coerce one, diminishing both awareness and true freedom of choice.

3. True intuition, coming from the Spirit makes no mistake and does not
   err, even though it may reveal things which we do not like and which
   may require of us sacrifices that we find very painful to make at
   this point. Thus should erroneous or evil promptings and "revelations"
   come, they cannot be from the intuition but must be from some other
   faculty and area of our being.

4. As the Spirit is not concerned with our own personal desires or welfare
   but with the true welfare and long-range good of humanity, intuition
   will generally not manifest itself for our personal benefit alone, but
   for the benefit of the group in which we operate.

5. True intuition always contains a bridge or connection between the
   inner and the outer world. Thus when it manifests we have both an inner
   subjective experience of well-being, a good conscience, a feeling of
   fullness and happiness, a true "inner peace" or harmony, which is
   matched by an outer recognition, by some people at least, even though
   it might generate some form of conflict at first which will later be
   recognized to be actually working out for the good of all concerned.

6. True intuition always manifests itself into the 3 great worlds of
   being: the superconscious world of the spirit, in terms of energies
   and promptings, the rational world of the personality, in terms of
   illumination and the highest and most exact reason, and the physical
   world in terms of some action or realization.

7. Should the "voice of intuition" not be recognized, or be recognized
   but not implemented to the best of one's abilities, it will remain
   silent for a while for the Divine Spark does not have "time or energies
   to waste" on instruments which are not ready to cooperate in the
   Great Work or who are too weak and disorganized to use effectively
   what has been freely given. The decision here is not ours but God's,
   i.e. it is that of the spiritual Self and not of the human self!

APPENDIX C

SYMBOLISM

Its Nature and Use

Symbolism is truly the "forgotten language" of our time, as one author put it; it is a forgotten language which, however, is fast being rediscovered and, again, explored and analyzed in depth by a growing number of thinkers in different fields. A number of world-renowned authors such as Jung, Fromm, Eliade, Campbell, Assagioli and others have dedicated a large part of their writings either attempting to define symbols and explaining their dynamics or using them and showing how other traditions and peoples have used them.

Until the Enlightenment symbols and myths made up one of the most important languages of humanity--its sacred language. During and after the Age of Reason until roughly WWII, this language fell in disuse and was slowly neglected and, consequently, no longer understood in its true nature and function. In the last 3 decades, however, it has again come to the foregound of our culture in transition and now commands more and more attention and investigation on the part of an increasing body of scientists, humanists, and writers. Today, we find again that some things can only be expressed in symbols and that some of the most ancient and deepest truths and principles were expressed in the language of symbolism, analogy, and myth rather than in the descriptive and analytical language of present day science.

Actually, there have always been 3 languages that human beings have used regardless of their linguistic tradition and of whether they spoke English, French, or Swahili. These 3 languages are:

a. The language of everyday speech which utilizes words as its units which are "handles" or instruments to convey and elicit thoughts and feelings. A word of everyday speech is thus said to have an intensive field made up of connotations and an extensive field made up of denotations.
b. The language of science which utilizes concepts as its units which are handles or media to convey and elicit thoughts (denotations) alone; ideas which are supposed to have an "empirical referens," i.e. that are capable of either observation or experience.
c. The language of poetry and religion, of the sacred traditions, which utilize symbols as their units which are handles or media through which thoughts, feelings, and intuitions are conveyed and elicited.

137

Thus one cannot read any of these 3 languages in the same way
without misunderstanding their true meaning and the way they are to be
used. It is this kind of confusion which has created countless conflicts and misunderstandings between religion and science during the last
5 centuries and which has brought about the devaluation and the demise
of religion in the modern world with very grave consequences for the well-
being of human beings as well as for our true understanding of both man
and the world, and of their creative source, the Spirit. The reason for
this is very simple: on the one hand, there has been in the Western
world a gradual but progressive evolution of reason with a concomitant
involution of emotion, imagination, instinct, and intuition. Thus symbols, which are the language of the irrational and superrational, were
interpreted more and more in a descriptive-analytical way, which is the
process by which the concepts of science are interpreted, rather than
in an analogical-allegorical way which is the process that should be
applied to symbols. The true meaning of symbols was thus lost and the
whole language degraded and neglected.

With the development of modern psychology, particularly depth
and height psychology, with the rediscovery and slow exploration of the
unconscious and then of the superconscious; with the anthropological
and ethnological studies of alien and exotic people of the Far-East,
of Africa, South America, and Polynesia; and with the surfacing again
of the sacred traditions in mysticism, occultism, and magic, it was
natural and inevitable the symbolism would be looked at more critically
and re-explored in its depths and potentialities. In the last 3 decades,
a certain consensus concerning the nature and functions of symbols has
been slowly emerging and has now crystallized in certain basic statements
and insights which are the following:

1. Symbols are the "language" and vehicles of the _irrational_ and _super-
   rational_--which are very different in their origins and nature--and
   not of the _rational_ part of man and of the world and life.
2. Symbols are the "language" and instruments of the unconscious and the
   superconscious rather than of the conscious.
3. Symbols are linked with the "right part of the brain" and with the
   "feminine principle" rather than with the "left part of the brain"
   and with the "masculine principle."
4. Symbols are connected with the "night-side of life" rather than with the
   "day-side of life" and with the "lunar" rather than with the "solar"
   principles.
5. In terms of the "functions of the psyche," symbols deal with the
   intuition, with _imagination_, and with _emotion_ rather than with _thinking_,
   sensations, or the _will_.
6. Symbols use the _analogical-allegorical_ method rather than the _descriptive-
   analytical_ one. This means that they have not one, socially standardized
   and well-defined, meaning but many meanings that are both personal and
   transpersonal; that they are not _static_ and _closed_ but rather _dynamic_
   and _open_ with ever-new emergent levels that come to the foreground as
   new layers and states of consciousness are activated; that they are
   based on the principle of _correspondence_ and _homology_ derived from the

great classical assumption that all things in the universe are
interrelated and that the microcosm (man) is a reflection of the
macrocosm (the world). This assumption was succinctly put in the
Hermetic axiom "As Above so Below." Thus while there are meanings
and correspondences of a given symbol that are known and agreed
upon; while some of its meanings are transpersonal or collective,
others are purely personal and must be interpreted from within
the context of their occurrence, the level of consciousness and
personal experiences of the person who is working with and using
it.

7. Unlike words and concepts, symbols are not "ready made"; they are
    a "mine" which must be mined, a seed which must be planted and allowed
    to grow to reveal its flowers and fruits. Symbols, in other words,
    demand a great deal of personal and conscious work through concen-
    tration, meditation, and contemplation, and they must be incarnated
    and rendered alive in the being and life of the person who used them.
    Their treasures and correspondences are never exhausted but continue
    to grow and to amplify as human experience is acquired and conscious-
    ness is altered and expanded. Because they function as "doors" of
    the psyche and as channels to connect the conscious with the uncon-
    scious and the superconscious, they can and should be used thousands
    of times with ever-new results and consequences.

8. Basically, symbols are used to create a bridge, a channel, or a
    connection between the field of consciousness and the unconscious and
    superconscious, between the personal and the transpersonal, between
    the profane and the sacred, so that the conscious and the known can
    expand and grow into the unconscious/superconscious and the unknown
    at its own speed and according to the level of readiness of the person
    who is using them.

9. Another interesting property of symbols is that they can both reveal
    and veil a certain reality or truth according to the level of con-
    sciousness and readiness of the person who is using them; and, likewise,
    they can both unite or synthesize different elements and levels or
    separate and dissociate them. For this reason, symbols have always
    been the "language of the sacred traditions and of the Mysteries,"
    revealing the inner truths to the Initiates and hiding them from the
    profane: expressing a fundamental truth or mystery on many different
    levels for different types of personality and of spiritual maturity.

10. While there is a practically infinite number of correspondences and
    associations which can be derived from symbols and to which they can
    apply, there are 3 basic dimensions to which they are generally applied:

    a. The historical-literal one: the meaning and association given
        to the symbol by its historical connection and its literal de-
        notation. Here what we have is the cultural "body" or embodiment
        of the symbol, its surface level which is still "raw" and un-
        developed, waiting to be developed and deciphered.

    b. The analogical-allegorical level applied to the microcosm, to man.
        Here the symbol is applied to man, to each human being, to his
        anatomy, physiology, or to some archetypal level of human experience.
        It must be developed, correlated, and properly applied to one self

and one's daily life. What is involved is the soul of the
symbol, which may or may not lead to its spirit, in one of its
major sets of correspondences and homologies.

c. The analogical-ontological level applied to the macrocosm, to
   the world.
   Here the symbol is applied to the world, the outer universe, and
   its anatomy, life, and unfoldment. It must also be developed,
   correlated, and properly applied to the world as one perceives,
   comprehends, and experiences it. What is involved is again the
   soul of the symbol, which may or may not lead to its spirit, in
   another major set of correspondences and homologies.

The general line of progression, in working with symbols, is to go
from the outer, exoteric, or historical-literal level to the analogical-
allegorical level as applied to the microcosm--which is the work of
the Lesser Mysteries, to the analogical-ontological level--which is
the work of the Greater Mysteries.

11. All symbols have a three-fold nature: a body, a soul, and a spirit.
    The body of the symbol is the symbol itself in its cultural mani-
    festation and embodiment--a letter, figure, sign, object, or gesture
    which stands for other things which must be discovered and experienced.
    Its soul is the many interpretations and sets of correspondences
    which can be linked with the symbol and discovered by working with
    it. The spirit of the symbol is the energy and life with which it
    is connected, the Spiritual Power, Being, or Process with which it
    is connected, and which one has to activate in oneself by identifying
    one's self with it.

12. All symbols also have a form or shape, a color or set of colors, and
    a name. To the form corresponds focalization and concentration, to
    the color various energies, and to the name, consciousness. Thus by
    working with a symbol, one has to focus one's attention and will upon
    a specific aspect, facet, or process of one's self, of the world, or
    of life; one has to invoke and experience certain energies; and finally,
    one has to identify and evoke a certain level of consciousness which
    will alter and transform the level of consciousness one is normally
    functioning in.

13. Symbols are thus the handles or psychic media which convey and elicit
    the various units of human consciousness which we call thoughts, feelings,
    vital energies, and intuitions. They are "streams of focused awareness,"
    bundles of energies, the lens which direct and focus our whole attention
    upon one aspect of Reality, whether outer or inner; they are catalysts
    which convey and awaken certain energies and states of consciousness
    in our own field of consciousness.

In short, they are the psychospiritual means by which we invoke a
certain presence, induce a certain state of consciousness, and focus
our awareness, by which we recreate, in ourselves, an image, facsimile,
or representation of that which is without or above us. They are the
means by which man can deliberately awaken and focus his thoughts,
feelings, energies, and intuitions by an effort of the will to link
his field of consciousness with something that stands outside, below,
or above that field of consciousness, thus expanding it and extending
it in ever-increasing syntheses.

They are, therefore, the key regulators and main switches of human consciousness and of man's inner life. It is through them that all alterations, focusing, and expansion of human consciousness takes place, for they are regulators, accumulators, and transformers of human consciousness. They enable man to temporarily connect himself, his field of consciousness, and to identify with something greater and larger than he is and thus to slowly transcend himself and actualize his latent energies, faculties, and potentialities. For it is a well known fact that the mind takes on the form of the object it beholds and that the vital energies of man will <u>run along the lines traced and focused upon by the mind and cathect or energize the things or areas about which man thinks.</u>

By way of a practical example, let us take the symbol of Christmas. At its historical-literal meaning, Christmas is the celebration of the birth of Jesus and the recalling of the main events that took place about 2,000 years ago in Bethlehem. This is the body of the symbol. One of its major sets of correspondences and meanings, or "soul," in the microcosm is the <u>blue-print</u> of every man's spiritual initiation which lies in <u>the future</u> and not in the past! Christmas here denotes the process and major events by which the spiritual Self of a human being becomes connected with his human self and is able to express and manifest Its life and attributes (Divine Wisdom, Divine love, and Divine Creative Energies) in one's field of consciousness and in the world. Moreover, by concentrating upon, meditating on, and contemplating this composite symbol we actually help to bring about its realization in ourselves, for all thoughts have a motor element or energy which seeks to realize and objectify itself in the physical world. Thus, far from being a purely passive experience relating to a past event, it becomes a creative process in which we have to involve all of the functions and faculties of our psyche to bring about its realization in the future.

How to work with symbols is both a science and an art; it involves a certain body of knowledge which has to be applied and certain practices which must be used and experienced in one's being and life. Briefly put, the basic way in which one works with symbols is the following: three major processes are involved: <u>concentration</u>, which focuses our consciousness through the use of the will, <u>meditation</u>, which uncovers and unveils its deeper meanings and correspondences, and <u>theurgy</u> which incarnates it and realizes its spirit in our being and life. Thus, we proceed in the following way:

1. We <u>concentrate</u> our whole attention upon the symbol we are working with to the exclusion of all other realities and things--we root our thoughts, feelings, energies, and intuitions upon it.
2. Then, through <u>reflective meditation</u>, we gather and bring into consciousness all the information, associations, and experiences we have had that are connected with this symbol. Then we empty our minds and practice <u>receptive meditation</u> to see if new meanings, insights, and correspondences will flow into our field of consciousness from the subconscious mind. Finally, we alter our state of consciousness through one of several techniques and use <u>contemplative meditation</u> to discover the essence and core of the symbol through the inspiration of the

superconscious mind and the revelations of the spiritual Self.
Lastly, we synthesize all of the knowledge and information gathered
so that we may now use it to incarnate and objectify it.

3. Finally, through <u>creative meditation</u> or <u>theurgy</u>, we seek to become,
   to act out, and incarnate what has been revealed to us through the
   foregoing process. We imagine that we <u>are</u> that which the symbol has
   revealed to us, we act "as if" we were that which the symbol has
   revealed to us, and finally, we slowly begin to alter our attitudes
   and behavior in the everyday world to conform to what the symbol has
   revealed to us, thus assimilating and incarnating it little by little.

Seen in this light, symbols are indeed a bridge or connection between
the known and the unknown, the conscious and the Deep Mind, actuality and
potentiality. They provide a blue-print by which we can progressively
transcend ourselves and become more than what we are. They form a graded
and progressive curriculum by which the Many can become the One, by which
the Profane can be linked with the Sacred, and by which the Supreme
Synthesis of finding union with God, or the fusion and alignment of the
human self with the Spiritual Self, can be realized--which is the true
purpose and destiny of <u>man</u> here on earth. As such, symbols are indeed
the "language of the sacred traditions" and the basic units through which
the <u>inner work</u> can be carried out and accomplished.

APPENDIX D

The Tree of Life and the Psychospiritual Centers

In several chapters of this book, I have mentioned the psychospiritual Centers of man's energy and consciousness fields. These
Centers, their nomenclature, nature, implications, and correspondences,
constitute a very important and fascinating, albeit complex and con-
troversial, subject matter that cannot adequately be covered in this
work. To do justice to this subject, another book is the minimum that
can be expected and which I already have in the planning stage for a
later time. In the Western Spiritual Tradition, this subject is related mainly to the Qabalah and the Ten Sephiroth of the Tree of Life.
In the East, on the other hand, it is related to the Chakras. Excellent
works have been published on this topic and can be consulted by the
interested reader. The ones that I am acquainted with and consider most
reliable, both in theoretical and in practical terms are:

Dion Fortune, The Mystical Qabalah, London: Ernest Benn, 1963.
Gareth Knight, A Practical Guide to Qabalistic Symbolism, London:
        Helios Book, 1965.
Z'ev ben Shimon Halevi, Tree of Life, New York: Weiser, 1973.
_____, Adam and the Kabbalistic Tree, New York: Weiser, 1974.
Israel Regardie, The Tree of Life, New York: Weiser, 1973.
William Gray, The Ladder of Lights, London: Helios Book, 1968.
R. G. Torrens, The Golden Dawn, New York: Weiser, 1973.
C. W. Leadbeater, The Chakras, London: Theosophical Press, 1938.

For the practical purposes of this work, I will include a basic diagram
of the Tree of Life and list the Hebrew and English names of the Centers
together with their most important meanings and correspondences.

The Tree of Life

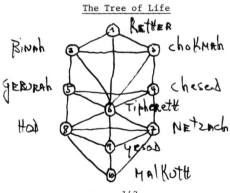

Name of the Centers	Location on human body	Astrological signs
1. Kether, The Crown	Head	Primum Mobile
2. Chockmah, Wisdom	Left Cheek	Zodiac
3. Binah, Understanding	Right Cheek	Saturn
4. Chesed, Mercy	Left Shoulder	Jupiter
5. Geburah, Severity or Strength	Right Shoulder	Mars
6. Tiphareth, Beauty or Equilibrium	Heart	Sun
7. Netzach, Victory	Left Hip	Venus
8. Hod, Splendor	Right Hip	Mercury
9. Yesod, Foundation	Genitals	Moon
10. Malkuth, Kingdom	Feet	Earth

Key Correspondences

1. Kether: Point of contact with the Divine Spark, Unity.
2. Chokmah: Eternal Masculine Principle, Expansion.
3. Binah: Eternal Feminine Principle, Contraction.
4. Chesed: Principle of expanding life, Energy, Enthusiasm.
5. Geburah: Principle of contracting life, Order, Discipline.
6. Tiphareth: Intuition, Equilibrium.
7. Netzach: Emotion, Combination.
8. Hod: Thought, Separation.
9. Yesod: Vitality, Creativity, Conception.
10. Malkuth: Behavior, Resolution.

Spiritual Experience, Virtue and Vice linked with given Center

1. Kether: Union with God; Completion of the Great Work; none.
2. Chokmah: Vision of God; Devotion; none.
3. Binah: Vision of Sorrow; Silence; Avarice.
4. Chesed: Vision of Love; Obedience; Tyranny, Hypocrisy.
5. Geburah: Vision of Power; Courage; Cruelty.
6. Tiphareth: Vision of Harmony; Devotion to Great Work; Pride.
7. Netzach: Vision of Beauty; Unselfishness; Lust.
8. Hod: Vision of Splendor, Illumination; Truthfulness; Falsehood, Dishonesty.
9. Yesod: Vision of the Machinery of the Universe; Independence; Idleness.
10. Malkuth: Vision of Holy Guardian Angel; Descrimination; Inertia.

The Tree of Life with its Ten Sephiroth has its roots and being in the Four Worlds of the Qabalists. These are:

Aziluth: Divine World; Divine Consciousness.
Briah: Mental World; Superconscious.
Yetzirah: Astral World; Conscious.
Assiah: Physical World; Unconscious.

The basic task of the student of the Mysteries is to become acquainted with the Tree of Life and each of its psychospiritual Centers; to cleanse, activate, and coordinate their energies so that these can be consciously used by the Self in man's consciousness and actions.

BIBLIOGRAPHY

A. Works focusing on humanistic and transpersonal psychology.

Assagioli, Roberto. Psychosynthesis: A Manual of Principles
    and Techniques. New York: Viking Press, 1965.

_____. The Act of Will. New York: Viking Press, 1973.

Dabrowski, Granger, et al (Editors). Psychotherapies
    Actuelles, Editions Saint-Yves Inc. Sainte-Foy, Q., 1977.

Harding, Esther, M. Psychic Energy: Its Sources and its
    Transformations. Princeton: Bollingen Paperback, 1973.

James, William, W. Psychology: Briefer Course. New York:
    Collier Books, 1962.

_____. The Varieties of Religious Experiences. New York:
    Modern Library, 1942.

Keyes, Ken. Handbook to Higher Consciousness. Berkley, CA,
    Living Love Center, 1974.

Lewis, Dennis. On the Way to Self-Knowledge. New York:
    Alfred Knopf, 1976.

Maslow, Abraham, H. Personality and Motivation. New York:
    Harper & Row, 1954.

_____. Towards a Psychology of Being. New York: Van
    Nostrand, 1968.

_____. The Farther Reaches of Human Nature. New York:
    Viking Press, 1971.

Ornstein, Robert, E. The Nature of Human Consciousness. New
    York: W. H. Freeman, 1973.

_____. The Psychology of Consciousness. New York: W. H.
    Freeman, 1972.

_____. On the Psychology of Meditation. New York: Viking
    Press, 1971.

145

Progoff, Ira. The Death and Rebirth of Psychology. New York: Julian Press, 1956.

_____. Depth Psychology and Modern Man. New York: McGraw Hill, 1959.

_____. The Symbolic and the Real. New York: Julian Press, 1963.

De Ropp, Robert, S. The Master Game. New York: Delta Book, 1966.

Singer, June. The Boundaries of the Soul. New York: Doubleday, 1973.

_____. Androgyny: Towards a New Theory of Sexuality. New York: Doubleday, 1976.

Tart, Charles (Editor). Altered States of Consciousness. New York: Doubleday, 1972.

Wilson, Colin. The Occult: A History. New York: Random House, 1971.

_____. New Pathways in Psychology. New York: Toplinger, 1972.

B. Works dealing with a synthesis of modern social science and esoteric, spiritual view-points.

Assagioli, Roberto. Martha and Mary. Kent, G. B.: Sundial House, 1975.

Bucke, Richard, M. Cosmic Consciousness. New York: Dutton & Co., 1969.

Eascott, Michal, J. The Silent Path. New York: Samuel House, 1973.

_____. Jacob's Ladder. Kent, G. B.: Sundial House, 1973.

_____. Invocation: Its Fundamentals and Practice. Kent, G. B.: Sundial House, 1973.

_____. Meditation and the Rhythm of the Year. Kent, G. B.: Sundial House, 1975.

Eascott, Michal & Magor, Nancy. The Plan and the Path. Kent, G. B.: Sundial House, 1975.

_____. Entering Aquarius. Kent, G. B.: Sundial House, 1975.

Eliade, Mircea. The Sacred and the Profane. New York: Harper Torchbook, 1959.

_____. Myths, Dreams, and Mysteries. New York: Harper Torchbook, 1957.

_____. The Two and the One. New York: Harper Torchbook, 1962.

Jones, Gladys, V. The Flowering Tree. La Canada, Ca.: New Age Press, 1972.

_____. Reincarnation, Sex and Love. La Canada, Ca.: New Age Press, 1971.

Leshan, L. The Medium, the Mystic, and the Physicist. New York: Viking Press, 1974.

Nouy, Lecomte du. Human Destiny. New York: Mentor Books, 1947.

Ouspensky, P. D. The Psychology of Man's Possible Evolution. Pondicherry, India: Sri Aurobindo Ashram, 1963.

Roche de Coppens, Peter. Spiritual Man in the Modern World. Washington: University Press of America, 1976.

Roszak, Theodore. Unfinished Animal. New York: Harper & Row, 1975.

Smith, Huston. Forgotten Truth: The Primordial Tradition. New York: Harper & Row, 1976.

Sorokin, Pitirim. The Crisis of our Age. New York: Dutton Paperback, 1941.

_____. The Ways and Power of Love. Boston: Beacon Press, 1950.

_____. Altruistic Love. New York: Kraus Reprint, 1969.

C. Works dealing with esoteric, occult, and mystical topics.

Butler, W. E. Magic: Its Ritual, Power, and Purpose. New York: Weiser, 1974.

_____. The Magician: His Training and Work. London: Aquarian Press, 1963.

_____. Apprentice to Magic. New York: Weiser, 1974.

Crookall, Robert. The Interpretation of Cosmic and Mystical Experiences. London: James Clarke, 1969.

Denning, Melita & Phillips, Osborne. The Magical Philosophy. 5 vols. St. Paul, Minn.: Llewellyn Publications, 1974.

Fortune, Dion. The Training and Work of an Initiate. New York: Weiser, 1976.

_____. Esoteric Orders and their Work. New York: Weiser, 1976.

_____. The Esoteric Philosophy of Love and Marriage. New York: Weiser, 1976.

_____. Applied Magic. New York: Weiser, 1973.

_____. Sane Occultism. New York: Weiser, 1973.

_____. The Goat Foot God. New York: Weiser, 1971.

Gray, William. Inner Traditions of Magic. New York: Weiser, 1970.

_____. Magical Ritual Methods. London: Helios Book, 1969.

_____. The Ladder of Lights. London: Helios Book, 1968.

_____. A Self made by Magic. New York: Weiser, 1976.

Halevi, Shimon Z'ev ben. Tree of Life. New York: Weiser, 1973.

_____. Adam and the Kabbalistic Tree. New York: Weiser, 1974.

Harley, Christine. The Western Mystery Tradition. London: Aquarian Press, 1968.

Iamblichus. On the Mysteries. Translated by Thomas Taylor. London: Stuart & Watkins, 1969.

Knight, Gareth. Experience of the Inner Worlds. London: Helios Book, 1975.

_____. The Occult. London: Kahn & Averill, 1975.

_____. A Practical Guide to Qabalistic Symbolism. 2 vols. London: Helios Book, 1965.

Regardie, Israel. The Tree of Life. New York: Weiser, 1973.

149

Regardie, Israel. Twelve Steps to Spiritual Enlightenment. New York: Weiser, 1973.

_____. The Middle Pillar. St. Paul, Minn.: Llewellyn Publications, 1970.

_____. The Art of True Healing. London: Helios Book, 1970.

Sadhu, Mouni. Concentration. Hollywood, Ca.: Wilshire Book, 1973.

_____. Meditation. London: George Allen & Unwin, 1969.

_____. Theurgy. London: George Allen & Unwin, 1965.

_____. Ways to Self-Realization. New York: The Julian Press, 1962.

Steiner, Rudolph. Knowledge of the Higher Worlds and its Attainment. New York: Anthroposophic Press, 1968.

_____. The Evolution of Consciousness. New York: Anthroposophic Press, 1966.

_____. The Stages of Higher Knowledge. New York: Anthroposophic Press, 1969.

_____. Education and Modern Spiritual Life. New York: Anthroposophic Press, 1968.

D. Works dealing with a mystical and spiritual view-point.

Bailey, Alice, A. The Soul and its Mechanism. London: Lucis Press, 1971.

_____. A Treatise on White Magic. London: Lucis Press, 1971.

_____. From Intellect to Intuition. London: Lucis Press, 1971.

_____. Education in the New Age. London: Lucis Press, 1971.

_____. Esoteric Psychology. 5 vols. London: Lucis Press, 1971.

Bergson, Henri. l'Evolution Creatrice. Paris: Felix Alcan, 1930.

_____. L'Energie Spirituelle. Paris: Felix Alcan, 1928.

Bergson, Henri. Les Deux Sources de la Morale et de la Religion. Paris: Felix Alcan, 1932.

Carrel, Alexis. L'Homme cet Inconnu. Paris: Librairie Plon, 1935.

_____. La Priere. Paris: Librairie Plon, 1944.

Chardin, Pierre Theilhard de. The Phenomenon of Man. New York: Harper Torchbook, 1964.

_____. The Future of Man. New York: Harper Torchbook, 1964.

Charidon, Igumen. The Art of Prayer, an Orthodox Anthology. Translated by E. Kadloubousky and E. Palmer. London: Faber & Faber, 1966.

Echartshausen, Karl von. The Cloud upon the Sanctuary. New York: SRIA 321 West 101st Street, 1952.

Heidel, Max. The Rosicrucian Cosmo-Conception. Oceanside, Ca.: Rosicrucian Fellowship, 1966.

_____. The Rosicrucian Christianity Lectures. Oceanside, Ca.: Rosicrucian Fellowship, 1955.

_____. The Rosicrucian Mysteries. Oceanside, Ca.: Rosicrucian Fellowship, 1966.

Lossky, Vladimir. The Mystical Theology of the Eastern Church. London: James Clarke, 1957.

Kopp, Joseph V. Theilhard de Chardin, a New Synthesis of Evolution. Glen Rock, NJ: Deus Book, Pauline Press, 1964.

Monk of the Eastern Church. On the Invocation of the Name of Jesus. London: The Fellowship of St. Alban and St. Sergius, 1960.

Papus. L'Occultisme. Paris: Robert Laffond, 1975.

_____. La Reincarnation. Paris: Editions Dangles, 1968.

Plummer, George W. Rosicrucian Fundamentals. New York: SRIA, 1920.

_____. Consciously Creating Circumstances. New York: SRIA, 1955.

Saint-Denis, Jean de. *Technique de la Priere*. Paris: Presence Orthodoxe, 1971.

_____. *Initiation a la Genese*. Paris: Presence Orthodoxe, 1971.

Sedir, Paul. *Initiations*. Paris: Bibliotheques des Amities Spirituelles, 1956.

_____. *La Priere*. Paris: Bibliotheques des Amities Spirituelles, 1955.

_____. *Les Guerisons du Christ*. Paris: Bibliotheques des Amities Spirituelles, 1953.

Sofrony, Archimandrite. *The Undistorted Image*. London: The Faith Press, 1958.

SRIA Documents, SRIA, 321 West 101st Street, New York, NY.

Underhill, Evelyn. *Mysticism*. New York: E. P. Dutton, 1919.

_____. *Worship*. New York: Harper & Brothers, 1937.

_____. *Practical Mysticism*. New York: E. P. Dutton, 1943.

BIOGRAPHICAL SKETCH

Peter Roche de Coppens was born in Vevey, Switzerland, on May 24, 1938. He was educated in Switzerland, Argentina and Italy through Secondary School and in the United States and Germany at the University level. He graduated with honors from Columbia University, was elected Phi Beta Kappa, and was the recipient of two Woodrow Wilson grants. He received his PhD from Fordham University in Sociology and is now a full professor of Sociology and Anthropology at East Stroudsburg State College. He is also an executive officer of the International Institute for Integral Human Studies in Montreal and the member of many other professional associations.

A productive writer and author Dr. de Coppens has published two books, Ideal Man in Classical Sociology (Pennsylvania State University Press, 1976) and Spiritual Man in the Modern World (University Press of America, 1976) as well as numerous articles in American and International journals.

For the last 20 years the leitmotiv of Dr. de Coppens has been the study of spirituality and the development of spiritual consciousness. He has travelled widely in many countries in search of the people and the information to enable him to pursue this interest at a serious level. He has personally known several mystics, scholars, and spiritually awakened people who provided him with a living model for his studies.

The present work represents, in his eyes, the crowning effort of his researches and experiments over the last 7-9 years and what he considers to be his major contribution to the study of spirituality.

36 63   2